TWAYNE'S WORLD AUTHORS SERIES
A Survey of the World's Literature

Sylvia E. Bowman, Indiana University
GENERAL EDITOR

SPAIN

Janet W. Díaz, University of North Carolina, Chapel Hill
Gerald Wade, Vanderbilt University
EDITORS

Gregorio and María Martínez Sierra

TWAS 412

Gregorio and María Martínez Sierra

GREGORIO AND MARÍA MARTÍNEZ SIERRA

By PATRICIA W. O'CONNOR

University of Cincinnati

TWAYNE PUBLISHERS

A DIVISION OF G. K. HALL & CO., BOSTON

Library of Congress Cataloging in Publication Data

O'Connor, Patricia Walker, 1931–
  Gregorio and María Martínez Sierra.

  (Twayne's world authors series; TWAS 412: Spain)
  Bibliography: p. 147–52.
  Includes index.
  1. Martínez Sierra, Gregorio, 1881–1947.
2. Martínez Sierra, María, 1880–1974.   3.   Authors,
Spanish — 20th century — Biography.
PQ6623.A82Z84   862'.6'2   76-45170
ISBN 0-8057-6252-3

to write a book . . .
to have a child . . .
to leave a memory . . .
PAX . . .

Contents

About the Author

Patricia W. O'Connor, Professor of Romance Languages and Literatures at the University of Cincinnati, has taught there since receiving her doctorate in 1962 from the University of Florida. She is active as officer and participant in regional and national professional associations and regularly contributes articles on contemporary Spanish theater and novel to scholarly journals. She is the author of the book *Women in the Theater of Gregorio Martínez Sierra* (American Press).

An enthusiastic supporter of study abroad, she directs the University of Cincinnati's academic programs in Spain and participated as an evaluator of summer programs in Spain in a recent two-year study sponsored by the American Association of Teachers of Spanish and Portuguese.

She is on the editorial staff of *Modern International Drama, Anales de la novela de posguerra* and *Hispanófila,* is co-editor with Anthony M. Pasquariello of Antonio Buero Vallejo's *El tragaluz* (Scribners), and since 1975 has devoted much time and energy to directing *Estreno*, a journal on contemporary Spanish theater.

Preface

When I undertook the writing of this book, originally entitled "Gregorio Martínez Sierra," I was, of course, familiar with the rumor that María had inspired or perhaps even written some of her husband's plays. As I searched through scholarly and journalistic criticism in search of evidence of her contribution, I found that while many critics mentioned María as a possible collaborator, no one had ever explored the nature of their working arrangement or had offered a shred of evidence to support the existence of a partnership. After María died in Buenos Aires (1974), numerous papers shipped to her family in Madrid were placed at my disposal. Among them, I found hundreds of letters from Gregorio, many newspaper clippings, telegrams, and other items which documented not only María's active writing role, but her exclusive authorship of much of what passes for the work of her husband. Representative excerpts from these papers are made public for the first time here (Chapter 2).

Although numerous stories, novels, essays, and poems bear the signature of Gregorio Martínez Sierra, it is as a dramatist and man of the theater that he will best be remembered. At the peak of his creative and physical powers (1915–1925), theater audiences marveled that he could write and produce several successful plays a year at the same time that he founded journals, directed publishing houses, managed an art theater, and toured the world as director of his repertory theater company. A partial solution to the apparent mystery is that Martínez Sierra was not one, but two enormously talented, disciplined and hard-driven individuals. While María devoted long hours to writing, Gregorio made suggestions (the reverse of their rumored roles) and oversaw the execution of the finished product. Although friends and theater professionals knew something of the nature and extent of María's involvement, the general public assumed that Gregorio was the author and that María, if anything, simply offered advice about the important feminine characterizations.

On occasion I employ the term "Martínez Sierra" (and subsequently "he") as the corporate symbol of this literary partnership. Because proof of her major contribution to the professional success of Gregorio Martínez Sierra is now available (photocopies on file in the University of Cincinnati Library), I have deliberately taken María out of the shadows to place her in the spotlight. Indeed, it is important to recognize María's achievement as a dramatist, for women the world over are notably absent from dramaturgy. The plays which María wrote alone and Gregorio signed alone (such was her desire) were enormously and consistently successful. This claim cannot be made in regard to any other Spanish woman dramatist, be she Gertrudis Gómez de Avellaneda, Emilia Pardo Bazán, Concha Espina, Julia Maura, or Ana Diosdado. María Martínez Sierra continues to be Spain's most successful woman dramatist.

In addition to shedding some light on the personal and professional partnership of the Martínez Sierras, I have reviewed what critics have written about them and their works. I have also examined the authors' works in the context of their literary era and their relevance for the contemporary reader. Unfortunately, because Martínez Sierra so thoroughly represented the artistic tastes of his day, some of his writings, particularly the early nondramatic works, have not withstood the test of time and are read very little. The feminist essays and plays as well as the dramas of maternal charity continue, however, to have relatively more universal application and appeal.

In Chapter 1, I have written of the lives of Gregorio and María and the circumstances surrounding the completion of several key works. For this information, I have relied heavily on María's book, *Gregorio y yo* and upon newspaper articles and interviews with surviving witnesses to the Spanish stage of the period. In the second chapter, I have dealt with the intriguing professional details of the literary collaboration and included further biographical data. Because the numerous novels and stories that the Martínez Sierras wrote between 1898 and 1910 are not only ignored but difficult to obtain, I have dealt with them rather extensively in Chapter 3. Although not particularly interesting in the literary sense, these works are nevertheless important in documenting the evolution of the Martínez Sierras from symbolic Modernistic dialogues to bourgeois commercial drama. In the following chapters, I explore the early theatrical works, the feminist plays, and finally the dramas of maternal nuns that have made the Martínez Sierra name world-famous.

Preface

I have elected not to deal critically with librettos composed for musical theater or with the many plays that Gregorio composed in collaboration with dramatists other than María (brief exception made in the special case of Santiago Rusiñol). Had space permitted, I would have written additional chapters on the feminist essays, the "triangle" plays, and several unpublished manuscripts. Some information, however, is included on all three of these areas.

I am deeply indebted to Margarita and Jaime Lejárraga, Catalina Bárcena, Catalina Martínez Sierra, Antonio Sempere, and several friends of Gregorio, María, and Catalina who generously shared with me invaluable information and insights. I should like to express my gratitude to Professors Anthony Pasquariello, John Kronik and Elizabeth Bettman for their thoughtful reading of certain chapters. I am also most grateful to Dr. Janet Díaz for her expert and efficient handling of the manuscript. While the suggestions of all these valued colleagues may account for much of what is meritorious in this book, they are in no way responsible for any lapses in fact or judgment.

Warm *abrazos* go to my daughter, Erin O'Connor, who showed budding editorial talent in reading a preliminary draft, and to Barbara Heisel for her help in the course of typing the manuscript.

And finally, I extend a special note of thanks to the members of the Charles Phelps Taft Memorial Fund Committee of the University of Cincinnati for their generous support of this research.

Chronology

1874　María de la O Lejárraga García is born in San Millán de la Cogolla, Spain. (Dec. 28)
1880　María's family moves to Madrid.
1881　Gregorio Martínez Sierra is born in Madrid. (May 6)
1897　Gregorio and María begin writing together.
1898　Gregorio begins the study of law at the University of Madrid but soon abandons these studies. Publication of *El poema del trabajo (Labor's Poem)*.
1899　Publication of *Diálogos fantásticos (Fantastic Dialogues)* and *Cuentos breves (Short Stories)*.
1900　Publication of *Flores de escarcha (Frost Flowers)* and *Almas ausentes (Absent Souls)*. Gregorio and María are married in Madrid. (Nov. 30)
1901　Gregorio founds literary journal, *Vida moderna (Modern Life)*.
1903　Gregorio and María join with Juan Ramón Jiménez, Pedro González Blanco and Ramón Pérez de Ayala to found the literary journal *Helios (The Sun)*.
1904　Publication of *Sol de la tarde (Afternoon Sun)* and *La humilde verdad (The Humble Truth)*.
1905　Publication of *Teatro de ensueño (Dream Theater)*. Gregorio and María travel to France, Belgium, England, and Switzerland. They write *Motivos (Motifs)*. *La humilde verdad (The Humble Truth)* wins a literary prize.
1906　Publication of *Tú eres la paz (You Are Peace)*. Performance of Martínez Sierra's translation of Rusiñol's *Buena gente (Good People)*.
1907　Performance in Madrid of *Vida y dulzura (Life and Sweetness)*, written in collaboration with Santiago Rusiñol. Publication of Gregorio's only volume of poetry, *La casa de la primavera (Springtime House)*. Gregorio founds literary journal, *Renacimiento (Renaissance)*.
1909　Performance of *La sombra del padre (Father's Shadow)*.
1910　Performance of *El ama de la casa (Mistress of the House)*. *El amor catedrático (Love Is the Teacher)* published.

1911   Performance of *Canción de cuna (Cradle Song)*, *Lirio entre espinas (Lily Among Thorns)*, *El palacio triste (The Sad Palace)*, and *Primavera en otoño (Autumn Spring)*.

1915   Performance of *Amanecer (Dawn)*, *El reino de Dios (The Kingdom of God)*, and *El amor brujo (Love's Sorcery)*.

1916   Performance of *Navidad (Holy Night)* and *El sombrero de tres picos (The Three-Cornered Hat)*, the latter with music by Manuel de Falla. Gregorio becomes artistic director of the Eslava Theater and forms the Compañia lírico-dramática Gregorio Martínez Sierra with Catalina Bárcena as lead actress. Publication of *Cartas a las mujeres de España (Letters to the Women of Spain)*.

1917   Publication of *Feminismo, feminidad, españolismo (Feminism, Femininity, Spanishness)*.

1918   Performance of *Sueño de una noche de agosto (Dream of an August Eve* or *The Romantic Young Lady)* and *Rosina es frágil (Rosina Is Fragile)*.

1920   Gregorio stages Federico García Lorca's first play, *El maleficio de la mariposa (The Spell of the Butterfly)*. Publication of *La mujer moderna (The Modern Woman)*.

1921   Performance of *Don Juan de España (Don Juan of Spain)*. *Cradle Song* performed in English at New York Times Square Theater.

1922   Daughter of Gregorio and Catalina Bárcena born in Madrid.

1924   Gregorio ceases to be director of Eslava Theater.

1925   Gregorio takes his dramatic company on tour of Europe and the Americas.

1927   Gregorio's theater company performs in New York (in Spanish).

1927   *Cradle Song* becomes the most popular repertory piece of Eva Le Gallienne. Performance of *Autumn Spring* in New York.

1929   Performance of *Seamos felices (Let's Be Happy)* in Madrid. Performance of *The Kingdom of God* in New York.

1930   Performance of *Triángulo (Triangle)* and *La hora del diablo (The Devil's Hour)*. *Sortilegio (Spell)* performed in Buenos Aires. English production of *Mamá (Mama)* at the Peacock Theater in London.

1931   Gregorio goes to Hollywood to supervise film versions of several works. *Madrigal* is performed in London by the New Players.

1932   Publication of *Nuevas cartas a las mujeres (More Letters to Women)*.

1933   María elected Granada's Socialist representative to the Cortes (Spanish Parliament). *The Romantic Young Lady* (translator's title for *Dream of an August Eve*) performed on Broadway. Ethel Barrymore performs *Cradle Song* and *The Kingdom of God* with much success. Paramount Pictures films *Cradle Song*.

1935   Gregorio returns to Spain to make the Spanish film version of *Cradle Song*.

1936   Outbreak of Spanish Civil War. The Republic assigns María as commercial attaché in Switzerland. Gregorio and Catalina Bárcena go to Buenos Aires.

1938   María settles in France (near Nice).

1942   Revival of *Spell* in Buenos Aires.

1947   Gregorio and Catalina return to Madrid in September. Gregorio dies of intestinal cancer (Oct. 1).

1952   María leaves from Geneva for New York and Hollywood.

1953   María settles in Buenos Aires. Publication in Mexico of *Gregorio y yo (Gregory and I)*.

1957   *Cradle Song* presented in New York at the Circle-in-the-Square Theater; also presented on NBC-TV starring Judith Anderson.

1964   Company of Manuel Callado revives *Triangle* with Catalina Martínez Sierra in one of the roles.

1974   María dies in Buenos Aires (June 28).

CHAPTER 1

Life and Times

G REGORIO Martínez Sierra, principally known for his work in the theater, early in his career combined the writing of novels, short stories, operettas, essays, and poetry with the translation of novels and plays into Spanish (mostly from French, English, Russian, and Catalan). The Sociedad General de Autores credits him with over two hundred titles including translations and adaptations but excluding the numerous critical and creative articles he contributed to periodicals. In addition to this copious literary production, Martínez Sierra directed *Vida moderna* (*Modern Life*), *Helios* (*The Sun*), and *Renacimiento* (*Renaissance*) — important literary journals that published the work of the major writers of the day — and founded the publishing houses Renacimiento and Estrella. In the period 1917–1930, he managed his own theater company (Compañía lírico-dramática Gregorio Martínez Sierra) and became Spain's outstanding theater director as well as its most prominent innovator. As an insistent apologist for a Theater of Art, he attempted to elevate the taste of Spanish audiences by introducing them both to great works of international theater and to new and experimental Spanish plays. He moved to Hollywood in 1930, believing that theater would succumb to the vital new industry of motion pictures. There he assisted in the preparation of films for Spanish-speaking audiences, rewrote several of his own plays for films (*Canción de cuna* [*Cradle Song*], *Mamá* [*Mama*], *Primavera en otoño* [*Autumn Spring*]), supervised their production and wrote original scripts for Metro-Goldwyn-Mayer, Paramount, and Fox Studios.

The fecundity and diversity of Martínez Sierra, playwright, novelist, essayist, poet, translator, journalist, adaptor, critic, editor, publisher, director, producer, businessman, and filmwriter are amazing, even when one takes into account that his name represents the combined work of not one but two enormously talented indi-

17

viduals of different yet compatible gifts: Gregorio and María Martínez Sierra. Although María and Gregorio worked independently in several areas, they collaborated in some fashion on all works published under his name.

I Historical and Literary Perspectives

In 1898, when Gregorio Martínez Sierra was seventeen and María de la O Lejárraga twenty-three, the literary Gregorio Martínez Sierra was born to Spanish letters via a slender volume of poetic dialogues entitled *El poema del trabajo* (*Labor's Poem*). That same year, the United States defeated Spain in the Spanish American War, thus writing a sad conclusion to an important chapter in Spain's history. In a scant three months, a youthful nation had stripped an aging one of important possessions abroad (Cuba, Puerto Rico, the Philippines, and one of the Marianas), thereby putting an end to an empire. This loss was the low point in a slide from world power that had begun in 1588 with the defeat of the Spanish Armada by the English.

While Spaniards of all classes shared the shock of defeat in 1898, intellectuals seemed to feel a particular sense of bewilderment and projected their special anguish in novels, poetry, theater, and essays, each writer seeking to isolate the virus of the nation's ills. A few even prescribed remedies, but most wallowed in frustration, anger, or wounded vanity.

Some writers (Pío Baroja, Valle-Inclán, Unamuno) pointed accusing fingers at the Church, the educational system, the military, the nobility, the uneven distribution of wealth, the decadent social structures, and a general national apathy they termed *abulia*. Other writers (Machado, Azorín, Maeztu, Ortega y Gasset, and again Unamuno) sought reassurance in the vigor of the stark Castilian countryside, the endurance of the common man, the changeless villages, and the timeless, universal importance of Spanish art. In search of seemingly lost identities and directions, a few (Maeztu, León, Espina) looked for Spain's authentic and peculiar genius in decisive moments of the past. They believed that Spain's failures derived from being disloyal to traditional virtues and goals; others, totally rejecting their ideas, looked for new models in Europe and the modern world in general (Costa, Ganivet and, in their early periods, Unamuno and Maeztu). Azorín gave this widely diverse group of sensitive, concerned, and essentially pessimistic patriots the title "Generation of '98."

Simultaneous with this intellectual renaissance directed by serious men of diverse ideology united in their concern for national problems, there existed yet another group of writers seemingly oblivious to the problems of Spain or the world. These writers disregarded parochial themes to fly to a cosmopolitan ivory tower of exotic beauty. Reacting against the pedestrian realism of the nineteenth century, they strove to create unusual metaphors, melodious rhythms and sensuous verbal imagery in pursuit of art, beauty, and grace. Following the lead of the French Parnassians, Symbolists, and Decadents — and led by Rubén Darío (Nicaraguan) and Juan Ramón Jiménez (Spanish) — these writers called themselves Modernists. Principally poets, they were the literary Bohemians of the Generation of '98, or, as some critics classify them, simply Modernists and a group apart.[1]

Modernism and the Generation of '98 form a literary Janus figure with one face gazing intently earthward at the soil of Spain (Generation of '98) while the gaze of the other (Modernist) is lost in ecstatic contemplation of the azure heavens and any form of beauty, real or imaginary. Major writers of the Generation of '98 were Miguel de Unamuno, Pío Baroja, Antonio Machado, Jacinto Benavente, Ramiro de Maeztu, Ramón del Valle-Inclán and Azorín, while the principal Spanish Modernists were Juan Ramón Jiménez, Salvador Rueda, Francisco Villaespesa, Eduardo Marquina, Ramón del Valle-Inclán, Manuel Machado and Gregorio Martínez Sierra. Benavente, Valle-Inclán and Martínez Sierra are sometimes classified with both groups, and Martínez Sierra, because of his late date of birth, is at times identified with the subsequent and more cosmopolitan generation, the *novecentistas*.

It was in the Modernist vein that Gregorio and María took their first literary steps. These early writings were full of allegory, metaphor, musical prose, exotic gardens, mythological wood creatures, pantheism, languid maidens, and Werther-like young men. The later works, however, more in line with the preoccupations of the Generation of '98, reflect a concern for Spanish cultural and social stagnation, especially in regard to women and the poor.

It was principally his work as an avant-garde, cosmopolitan theater director (Eslava Theater, 1917–1924) that aligned Gregorio with the universal and intellectual concerns of the *novecentista* group.

Although never an active politician or Socialist as was María, Gregorio firmly believed in equality of education for all and defended the rights of women to assert themselves professionally as well as personally. Their gentle blend of revolution as regards women and the disadvantaged occupies an important place in the many works they wrote together.

II   Life of Gregorio Martínez Sierra

While both María and Gregorio Martínez Sierra enjoyed happy childhoods and were the eldest of large, middle-class families (he of nine and she of eight children), their formative years differed considerably. Gregorio's forebears, for example, were merchants and industrialists, while hers were scientists and intellectuals. Although reared in a traditional bourgeois home, Gregorio was considerably influenced by his progressive, energetic, and gifted maternal grandfather. Enormously interested in electricity and its possible uses in Spain, the elder Sierra made regular trips to France to learn the latest developments in this area. He established the first electrical company in Madrid, installed the equipment in the Royal Palace, and invented a telegraph service that the Spanish army employed for many years.

Young Gregorio not only admired his grandfather but actively cultivated and emulated him. On Sundays, which the family spent in his company, Gregorio regularly offered ten céntimos to the brother or sister who spoke least. In this way, Gregorio was able to dominate the attention and conversation of the admired relative, who in turn doted on the eldest grandchild. This thirst for knowledge and progress was apparently lacking in Gregorio's parents, who, according to María, bought no books other than texts for the children and read only ultraconservative journals.[2] Gregorio's mother was, in María's view, a puritanical, fanatical Catholic who opposed all frivolity and attempted to instill in her first-born her own unquestioning faith.[3] Despite — or perhaps because of — her efforts, Gregorio early rejected, on a conscious level at least, all belief in the supernatural aspects of religion.

Of the nine children in the Martínez Sierra family, it was Gregorio who gave promise from a young age of achieving important things in life. Although of a timid, melancholy, and retiring disposition, he possessed great curiosity coupled with a tremendous desire to accomplish the goals he set for himself.

It was through his grandfather that Gregorio first became acquainted with the theater. The Sierra Electric Company had installed the electrical equipment in the Comedia Theater and provided a technician on the premises for all performances. On Sundays, the employee assigned to the theater customarily took the owner's grandson with him to view the performance from the prompter's box. It was here, no doubt, that young Gregorio began to absorb a feeling for dramatic technique and stage action.

As a hobby Gregorio began to write dialogues based on stories he read, and at the age of ten, using young friends as actors, produced and directed his version of Defoe's *Robinson Crusoe* for neighborhood friends.[4] Although Martínez Sierra characteristically preserved his works in a meticulous way, this manuscript, along with several other early compositions, was lost in the chaos of the Spanish Civil War.

Gregorio was always an avid reader. During his high school years at the Liceo Francés, he read plays by Corneille and Racine with great interest and spent vacations in France. The influence of French literature and the discipline acquired in the liceo were, no doubt, important factors in his cultural formation. In addition to Classical French writers, he was especially fond of the delicate imagery of Maurice Maeterlinck (1862–1949), the Belgian poet and dramatist. The Martínez Sierras would one day translate into Spanish his entire works in a five-volume edition.

At the age of fourteen, Gregorio organized his first amateur acting troupe and named it El Porvenir (The Future). For these performances, Gregorio adapted dialogue from novels.[5] It was during this period, perhaps, that theater ceased to be simply a pastime. In any case, these early theatrical activities served as the practice ground for the brilliant producer, stage director, and creator of dialogue that Martínez Sierra would one day be. Although he did not become director of Madrid's Eslava Theater until the age of thirty-five (1916), the embryonic impresario-director was already quite apparent in the adolescent Gregorio.

After graduation from high school, Gregorio traveled in France and England. He already spoke fluent French from his experience at a French school; at this time he learned English. In the fall of 1898 he entered the University of Madrid, but failure in a course on the critical history of Spain discouraged him and caused him to abandon university studies. "At this point," he confesses, "I coughed dreadfully and life was gray. I had no doubt that I was destined to die young and sad. But the tenacious will of a woman gently diverted the wheel of fate, and I stopped coughing and learned to laugh. I dreamed of writing verses full of music and mythological figures. I really saw nymphs behind every tree and nyads in each drop of water."[6]

III *Life of María Martínez Sierra*

The tenacious woman to whom Gregorio referred was María de la O Lejárraga, born in San Millán de la Cogolla on December 28, 1874 but reared in Madrid. María's childhood home, unlike Gregorio's, overflowed with books on science, history, philosophy, and literature, and she was encouraged to read and challenge any statements or beliefs therein espoused. Much like Gregorio, she had fallen in love with the theater at an early age (six) after seeing in Madrid's Teatro Español *La pata de la cabra* (*The Goat's Foot*), a fantasy in which people and tables floated miraculously through the air. After seeing this performance, she constantly dreamed of the theater, and her favorite toy became a cardboard stage with puppets she could move and through whom she could speak.[7]

Despite María's liberal upbringing, she was a pious Catholic until well into her twenties, when one by one she began to reject conventional Catholic beliefs. Curiously enough, in early adulthood, María, who was brought up to doubt, believed, while Gregorio, reared to accept faith without question, rejected traditional religion. When María and Gregorio first met, her faith was still intact while Gregorio's did not emerge until late in life, and then only in a perfunctory fashion.[8] This lack of religious accord was one of the few blights on an otherwise harmonious union during the early years of their relationship. Despite Gregorio's rationalistic rejection of religion, his subconscious retained the early teachings for some time, for frequently he would awaken from the recurring nightmare that he had been thrust into hell for his sins.[9]

IV *The Early Collaboration*

After graduation from high school, María attended the Normal School in Madrid to become a language teacher. Although she had known Gregorio for years as a friend of her younger brothers, they became special friends at summer dances in Carabanchel where both families were vacationing in the summer of 1897. Too timid, perhaps, to dance with girls of his own age, Gregorio sat with María, already a teacher of French, English, and Italian in Madrid and six and a half years his senior. Partly because both had an avid interest in literature, particularly the theater, their relationship flourished. They soon joined forces on literary projects and married largely as a result of the harmonious collaboration.[10]

Before the wedding in November 1900, the couple had published five works composed jointly: *El poema del trabajo* (*Labor's Poem*, 1898), *Diálogos fantásticos* (*Fantastic Dialogues*, 1899), *Cuentos breves* (*Short Stories*, 1899), *Flores de escarcha* (*Frost Flowers*, 1900) and *Almas ausentes* (*Absent Souls*, 1900). The last, a short novel, won for them a one thousand peseta prize (quite a sum in 1900) which provided the item of highest priority in their first home: a heater.[11] Because both had suffered enormously from the cold winters in Madrid, this stove was a treasured luxury later recalled with much nostalgia. Their distaste for the cold may also explain the obsession with the sun and warm climates apparent in the early works.

It was through the intercession of Benavente that Martínez Sierra's first book, *Labor's Poem*, was published.[12] Benavente, Spain's major dramatist, became a personal friend and helped Gregorio's career whenever possible. Another important professional and personal influence — perhaps the most important in the lives of Gregorio and María — was that of Juan Ramón Jiménez, the leading Modernist poet, whom they probably met in 1900 when he visited Madrid. That year, Juan Ramón dedicated the poem "Tarde gris" ("Gray Afternoon") to Gregorio and two years later dedicated a nocturne from *Rimas* (*Rhymes*) to his young friend. Following the then popular literary practice of "supportive criticism," Martínez Sierra published an enthusiastic review of *Rhymes*.

During the first few years of the twentieth century, Gregorio followed another custom common to the literary groups: he sat with other fledgling writers for long hours of discussion in the *tertulias* (social gatherings) presided over in the coffee houses and taverns by established writers. Each *tertulia* became something of a fraternity in the sense that the same people attended regularly.

The early years of Gregorio and María's marriage were happy and filled with hopes for the future. María provided the major support for the couple by teaching in a working-class district in Madrid.

Here she saw poverty first-hand. On one occasion, María was particularly impressed with her students' response to an assignment in which they wrote about an imaginary happy day. Most dreamed of eating meat, fish, potatoes, ham, and bread. She agonized then that many children went to bed hungry.[13] Although the experience did not move her to political action during this particular period, the memory remained with her, nurturing her reformist leanings later in life when time and inclination led her to Socialism and an active role in government.

While María taught, Gregorio did editorial work and tried to establish himself in the literary world. He initiated the short-lived Modernist literary journal, *Vida moderna (Modern Life)* in 1901, but it lasted only four issues. In 1903, Gregorio and María founded, with Juan Ramón Jiménez, Ramón Pérez de Ayala and Pedro González Blanco, *Helios*, a journal that would publish works by unknown writers as well as established ones.[14] The format of the publication was modern, bold, and elegant. Other contributors to the journal were Benavente (whose *La noche del sábado* was first published in *Helios*), the Quintero brothers, Emilia Pardo Bazán and Juan Valera. Despite its artistic success, this journal went out of existence in 1904 after fifteen issues. Helios, "the sun," continued in the literary works of Gregorio and María, however, for among the stories and novels published that year (1904) were: *Sol de la tarde (Afternoon Sun), Horas de sol (Sunny Hours)* and "Golondrina de sol" ("Sunny Swallow"). In 1904 they also published *La humilde verdad (The Humble Truth)*, a novel which won third prize in a literary contest for which it was written.[15]

In 1904, a very active year, Gregorio submitted *Mamá (Mama)* to a drama contest on whose panel of judges sat a friend, novelist Benito Pérez Galdós. Although theoretically the judges were unaware of the authors of works under consideration, Galdós called the Martínez Sierras to say that he favored their play and believed that it would win the prize if they were willing to make some modifications in the script within twenty-four hours. Galdós was particularly enchanted with their feminine protagonist, whom he termed "the most authentic woman"[16] of the contemporary theater. Although Gregorio and María agreed to the changes and spent the entire night implementing them, *Mama* failed to win the contest. The judges declared, in fact, that no play submitted showed sufficient quality to merit the prize. Curiously enough, *Mama* and two other plays (one by Eduardo Marquina and another by Linares Rivas) presented to this particular contest were subsequently performed in the Princess Theater by the Guerrero-Mendoza Company with brilliant success.

In 1905, doctors warned María that Gregorio, coughing excessively, would succumb to the active tuberculosis of several members of his family if he did not leave Madrid immediately for a warmer climate. (Five brothers and a sister died of tuberculosis within two years). María cast about for a way she and Gregorio could go abroad for an extended trip. Because neither had skills other than literary ones, María decided to apply for a scholarship that the Normal School offered annually to one of its graduates for the study of pedagogy in another country. She still had to convince her husband, however, that they should give up their work in Madrid for such a venture, for Gregorio's writing career was now progressing nicely. In addition, because Gregorio had a morbid fear of death, she dared not tell him the true reason for the trip.[17] She let him think that the requested hasty departure was partly a feminine whim to which he must succumb. María complained to Gregorio that she had been working very hard and that if she did not get away for some rest and sunshine, she would surely become tubercular. Sympathetic to her plea, Gregorio agreed to the trip. In this situation, María functioned much like their future heroines of the theater: these basically maternal women have their way but use attractive feminine wiles more than reason, petulance, or tears to accomplish their purpose. In her tactics, María also recalls the early Nora of Ibsen's *A Doll's House*, a work she would translate and Gregorio would perform in the Eslava Theater with Catalina Bárcena (the actress for whom Gregorio ultimately left María) in one of the most triumphant roles of her career.

Before leaving Spain, the Catalan publishers Montaner and Simón, impressed with *The Humble Truth*, asked Martínez Sierra to compose a novel of a specific length for which they would pay the then handsome fee of fifteen hundred pesetas. The only proviso other than length was that the novel, destined to form part of a collection geared to the family market, be "of absolute morality." Gregorio agreed to the terms and left for Paris. It was in a modest Parisian pension that the couple wrote the requested "moral" novel, *Tú eres la paz (You Are Peace)*, a sentimental work that would become a special favorite of romantic young women in South America and in Spain.[18]

The Paris trip, undertaken for reasons of health, turned out to be very profitable professionally. There they became friends of Santiago Rusiñol (Catalan dramatist), Albéniz and de Falla (Spanish musicians), Eduardo Marquina (Spanish poet and dramatist), and the elder Garnier (head of the famous French publishing house of the same name). Rusiñol, Albéniz, de Falla, and Marquina would, in years to come, collaborate with the Martínez Sierras on important works, and in 1905 Garnier would publish some of Gregorio and María's writings: *Granada, Motivos (Motifs)* and *La feria de Neuilly (The Neuilly Fair)*. María also translated Stendhal's *Le Rouge et le noir* into Spanish for Garnier.

After several happy, active and productive weeks in Paris, Gregorio decided to return to Madrid with Santiago Rusiñol, who tempted him with the possibility of having a play performed in the Comedia Theater. There was no danger in Gregorio returning to Spain now, because his health had improved, and the cold weather had passed. María, alone for the first time since her marriage — perhaps for the first time in her life — accepted disappointment stoically and learned to be self-sufficient.

María remained several more months in Paris studying and writing before Gregorio rejoined her in 1906 after collaborating with Rusiñol on the Castilian version (Rusiñol wrote only in Catalan) of the Catalan dramatist's *Buena gente (Good People)*. After further travel in France, England, Belgium, and other countries, Gregorio and María returned to Spain to pursue their dramatic career in earnest.

Martínez Sierra's first performed play was *Vida y dulzura (Life and Sweetness*, 1907), written with Santiago Rusiñol. Of their collaboration, María explains: "After having divided the work, planned the play, and decided on the order of the scenes, we set up our work areas in three adjoining rooms. Rusiñol wrote in Catalan; we wrote in Spanish. We communicated to each other our respective 'fruits' and argued, approved, disapproved, cut, changed, and added with absolute impartiality, good humor, and perfect harmony. When we had finished the bilingual work, Rusiñol translated into Catalan our Spanish, and I put into Spanish his Catalan; thus that happy product of three minds was born speaking two languages."[19] *Life and Sweetness* opened simultaneously in Madrid and Barcelona. (The Catalan version was entitled *Els savis de Vilatrista*). In Madrid, Rosario Pino, Benavente's favorite actress, starred in this work which was well received by critics and public alike. Martínez Sierra now had at least part of a commercial success to his credit, and if the doors of the theater were not exactly wide open, they were no longer locked tight. This same year, 1907, marked the publication of Gregorio's volume of poetry, the only work bearing his name in which María figures exclusively as muse rather than active collaborator or sole author. He called this book of homey verses about his own married happiness *La casa de la primavera (Springtime House)*, a title suggested by Juan Ramón Jiménez. Also in 1907, Gregorio founded another literary journal, this one entitled *Renacimiento (Renaissance)*.

V *Gregorio Meets Catalina Bárcena*

Ironically enough, about the time Gregorio was publishing his songs of domestic bliss, he met Catalina Bárcena, a young, Cuban-born actress in the theater company of María Guerrero and her husband, Fernando Díaz de Mendoza. Catalina had made her theatrical debut as Coralito in the Quinteros' *El genio alegre (The Happy Genius*, 1906) and in 1908 enjoyed rather spectacular success as doña Sol in Eduardo Marquina's *En Flandes se ha puesto el sol (The Sun Has Set in Flanders)*. When she became pregnant (the year is uncertain, but approximately 1908–1910), she married Ricardo Vargas, a fellow actor in the company. Catalina and her husband never lived together for any length of time, and fellow actors believed her son, Fernando Vargas, to be the child of Fernando Díaz de Mendoza.

Catalina Bárcena, a fragile and shy beauty, used her acting roles as masks to hide her timidity more than as vehicles of attention and actually came to theater more by default than design.[20] Since she had successfully acted in school, she continued acting because opportunities presented themselves. She had enormous talent — if not ambition — and Gregorio, recognizing her tremendous natural gifts, provided the direction. He became for her over the years a professional mentor as well as the love of her life. Under Gregorio's guidance, Catalina became a leading Spanish actress in the years 1915–1930.

At about this time, Martínez Sierra also became friendly with Serafín and Joaquín Álvarez Quintero, the dramatist brothers whose names were magic in commercial theater circles. It was through their influence that *La sombra del padre (Father's Shadow)* was performed. It enjoyed moderate success in Madrid but fared better in the provinces. In any case, the play solved the pressing economic problems of Gregorio and María for 1909, at least.

After the success of *Father's Shadow*, Gregorio asked María if she would like to take a trip to Italy. María, always eager to travel, responded affirmatively. Because the suggestion came from Gregorio, generally unwilling to abandon familiar surroundings for the discomfort of travel, one suspects (especially when we know of María's account of her trip), that perhaps Gregorio was simply anxious to have his wife out of Madrid; he was probably already much interested in Catalina Bárcena. In 1908, he was, at any rate, preparing a play for her, *Primavera en otoño (Autumn Spring)*, the first Martínez Sierra play in which she would perform. When time for the trip to Italy arrived, Gregorio suggested that María go ahead without him and that he would join her in two weeks.

In *Gregory and I*, María tells of stopping at a Barcelona beach on her way to Italy and of being mesmerized by the sound of the waves. Apparently in a trance, she entered the water but suddenly was startled by a rock splashing at her feet. The man who threw the rock begged her pardon and explained that he was afraid she was about to commit suicide. As she left the beach, she thought to herself, "I believe that I had no conscious intention of committing suicide, but if that man hadn't thrown the rock, I would surely have drowned myself."[21]

That María did not mention any depressing thought (indeed perhaps she was not even consciously aware of one) as she recounts the episode in Barcelona is not surprising; María had a penchant for suppressing all unpleasantness. There were, however, potentially depressing factors in María's life in 1909: (1) she had borne no children in nine years of marriage; (2) she was losing her husband to another woman. Indeed, when Gregorio finally left María to live with Catalina Bárcena (approximately 1922), María may have suffered a double loss. Many believe that Gregorio, in addition to being a husband, was María's surrogate child.

Although María stated many times that she never wanted a flesh-and-blood child and that she was quite satisfied with her "literary offspring," her family felt that not having children was one of María's bitterest disappointments. Despite her writing: "Never, never, not even in the most deeply felt 'trance' of love have I dreamed of having in my arms a child of my flesh and my blood,"[22] her statement rings false when one considers the many works she either inspired or wrote in which maternity was lyrically praised as woman's loftiest expression. Another irony in connection with María's stated disinterest in children (of her own) was a long-standing and insistent rejection of dolls. Moreover, her pet name for Gregorio, used frequently in correspondence, was *muñeco* ("doll"). Despite María's early and consuming interest in puppets, she makes several references to her dislike of dolls and relates on several occasions that her only interest in them was to tear them apart to see what was inside.[23] This rejection of dolls and assumed corollary lack of maternal instinct, reiterated too often to have been a mere casual or thoughtless comment, seems contradictory and defensive. Indeed, the endearing term "doll" for Gregorio either gives lie to her rejection or suggests some anger on her part for Gregorio. In the light of their lives and María's custom of keeping things to herself, such hostility would hardly be surprising.[24]

VI *Conception of* Cradle Song

After stopping briefly in Barcelona, María continued on to Nice and Florence where she spent a month alone — rather than two weeks — visiting museums and churches and absorbing Italian painting. After Gregorio arrived, the couple saw more Italian art. In a sense, it was the constant visual absorption of images of the Virgin and Child, portrayed in countless styles and attitudes, that prepared the way for *Cradle Song.* The minimal action for the play was suggested in an Italian newspaper story that María noticed and related to Gregorio: a newborn baby had been abandoned beside the baptismal font of a church. When María commented that in Spain the baby would have been left in the turnshelf of the convent, Gregorio suggested that a baby left to nuns might serve as material for a dramatic scene. At first, neither could see how such a subject could develop beyond one act, and they needed a two-act play if they wanted to open in the Lara Theater. Intermittently during the rest of the trip, Gregorio and María spoke of the possibilities suggested in the reactions of nuns to finding a baby left to them. Finally one of the two (María does not recall which) suggested that the first act could feature the reactions of the nuns to the baby; the second act could show the child as a young woman about to leave her "mothers." Because they liked the possibilities of the theme more and more, Gregorio and María set to work, while still traveling, on the play that would establish their fame and fortune in the theater and become a classic in modern international repertory.

Cradle Song was two years in gestation. In addition, the original title, "Maternidad" ("Maternity"), was abandoned when it was learned that the French dramatist, Brieux, already had a play by that name.[25] The work did not acquire its final title until after completion. "Cradle Song" was taken from a line of the Intermission poem that summarizes progress between acts and delicately accentuates the theme of the play.

When the Martínez Sierras returned from Italy, they continued to work on Cradle Song as they offered theater managers El ama de la casa (Mistress of the House). Reception to the script was cool, and even Gregorio and María were dubious about the possibilities of success. Action was minimal, and the play featured neither Benavente's incisive wit nor the Quinteros' humor. The Quintero brothers read Mistress of the House, believed in its possibilities, and more generous than some with potential competition, used a little blackmail to accomplish acceptance. They informed the Lara Theater manager: "If you want us to give you our play this year, and it is already written, you will have to perform Martínez Sierra's play first."[26] Since the theater needed the financial assurance of a Quintero play, Mistress of the House was performed, and with a success that amazed the authors as much as anyone. Amidst the prosperity of this work, María optimistically gave up teaching to devote herself entirely to literary collaboration with Gregorio.

By 1911, Martínez Sierra had two moderately successful plays to his credit and with a certain assurance took his new play, Cradle Song, to the Lara Theater. The impresario, however, after reading it was frankly dismayed. How, he asked Gregorio, could he stage a work, with little plot and no starring role, about cloistered nuns who squabbled, licked cookie pots, and stuck their tongues out at one another?[27] The Spanish public, accustomed to action, to the star system, and to nuns portrayed as mystical, romantic creatures, would surely reject this kind of piece as dull as well as irreverent. Because Benavente and the Quintero brothers were enthusiastic about the play, the Lara Theater management ultimately agreed to undertake production.

On opening night, Gregorio nervously encouraged the actresses behind the scenes while María, always fearful on such occasions, watched the professional debut of her most famous child from the audience. She was especially happy to see that not only women took out their handkerchiefs in the course of the play, but many men as well.[28] At the conclusion of the performance, Gregorio received a standing ovation as did Leocadia Alba, who played the role of the vicaress. After the success of *Cradle Song*, Gregorio no longer had to plead with impresarios to perform his works; he was now courted by them.

A few weeks after the opening of *Cradle Song*, Gregorio became gravely ill with typhoid fever. The rumor even circulated in Madrid that he had died. The gravity of his illness, María modestly suggests, may have influenced somewhat the concession of the Royal Academy's prize for the best work of that year to *Cradle Song*.[29]

The next few years were full of professional triumphs. The Martínez Sierras wrote a series of successful plays in which Catalina Bárcena starred as they collaborated with Spanish musicians to produce musical theater. The most important of their musical collaborators, Manuel de Falla, became a warm personal friend (especially of María) and lived with the couple for a year during this period (approximately 1914). In 1915 *El amor brujo (Love's Sorcery)* was performed, followed in 1916 by *El sombrero de tres picos (The Three-Cornered Hat)*. These two works, for which de Falla wrote the music, continue to be performed regularly and successfully in various parts of the world. Indeed, they enjoy an honored position in international musical theater repertory.

VII   The Gregorio Martínez Sierra Theater Company

In 1915 and 1916, Gregorio took several of his works on a tour of the Spanish provinces with Catalina Bárcena and Enrique Borrás as stars. In 1916, he formally constituted his own theater company, Compañía lírico-dramática Gregorio Martínez Sierra, with Catalina as lead actress. Although Catalina was a major drawing card, this collaboration, like the literary one with María, bore only Gregorio's name. He established his base of operations in the Eslava Theater, just off the Puerta del Sol in Madrid. For eight years (1916–1924), Gregorio would perform many of his own works in this theater, but he sought also to raise the level of sophistication of audiences and expand their theater tastes. He exposed them, at any rate, to an internationally classical and modern repertory as well as to avant-garde works by Spanish authors. During this period, the Eslava became the center of theatrical experimentation in Spain.

Although American Hispanists remember Martínez Sierra principally as the author of realistic, optimistic, and sentimental plays about women, theater people in Spain remember him as an outstanding, creative and innovative director of Madrid's only art theater for nearly a decade. It was he who separated direction of the actors from staging and set design — all three tasks usually performed by the lead actor or actress — and brought such outstanding artists to the Spanish theater as Manuel Fontanals, Rafael Barradas and Siegfredo Burman. Between 1917 and 1924, the Eslava Theater under his direction was compared to L'Oeuvre, the Paris art theater, and Martínez Sierra acquired an international reputation as director. He was compared to such immortals as Mayerhold, Stanislavsky, Fortuny, Fuchs, Lugne-Poë, and others.[30] During this important period of the Eslava Theater, Martínez Sierra directed works by Shakespeare, Molière, Goldoni, Dumas, Ibsen, Moreto, and Marquina and introduced George Bernard Shaw, James Barrie, and others to Spanish audiences.

He also opened the door of the Eslava to young, unknown Spanish dramatists, many of whom would one day vindicate his faith in their budding talents. He staged Federico García Lorca's first play, *El maleficio de la mariposa* (*The Spell of the Butterfly*, 1920), when Lorca was just over twenty. Although Catalina Bárcena and the dancer La Argentinita played lead roles in this work directed by Martínez Sierra (featuring the unusual set designs of Migoni and costuming by Barradas), the first-night audience received it rudely with traditional signs of displeasure: hissing and stomping. Other members of the avant-garde yet heterogeneous group of authors whose first works were rejected by other theaters but performed by Martínez Sierra at the Eslava include: Concha Espina, Honorio Maura, Felipe Sassone, Manuel Abril, Jacinto Grau (although Martínez Sierra did make the mistake of rejecting Grau's *El señor de Pigmalión*), Juan Antonio Luca de Tena, Tomás Borrás and others.

VIII *Separation*

With financial and artistic victories came personal disappointments for María. As Catalina Bárcena became more and more important in Gregorio's life, María did more writing alone. Gregorio shifted his collaboration to Catalina and, in effect, masterminded her career while María became the literary Martínez Sierra. Although some believe that Gregorio left María for Catalina about the time *Cradle Song* (1911) was on the boards, such is not the case. For many years Gregorio maintained the appearance of a normal marriage, superficially at least. It was during this period, though, that María turned her attentions and passions to the international feminist movement and wrote several volumes of essays on the rights and responsibilities of modern women.[31] It is interesting to note that one of the basic tenets of her equality program was that both men and women adhere to the stricter moral standards established for women rather than permit women the freedom theoretically allowed men. In regard to her personal situation, she would then require the absolute fidelity of Gregorio rather than permit herself the freedom of taking a lover. Such may have been her tacit message to Gregorio, for apparently she was unable to give the message directly.

At least one critic relates María's apparent acceptance of Gregorio's involvement with Catalina to her feminism. Showing some hostility to María, whom he calls "leftist and unfeminine," he believes that she flaunted her feminism by approving of her husband's right to take a lover.[32] While María could hardly have approved — either personally or as a feminist — of Gregorio's involvement with Catalina, she did maintain a reserve that may have suggested tacit consent to some. This critic also believes that the marriage of Gregorio and María was a Platonic relationship based exclusively on literary interests. In an interview in Buenos Aires, however, María makes a statement that would seem to refute such an opinion. Her illustrative anecdote may also shed some light on Gregorio's personality and somewhat parasitic relationship with women. In answer to the interviewer's question: "Was your marriage exclusively intellectual?" María responded: "Absolutely not. We married very much in love and after a long engagement. I remember that after the wedding we went up to the rooms that I had in the City School of Madrid where I was a teacher. There were some very long and steep stairs. When we got to the top, we hugged each other, and do you know what we said in unison? As if we had had the same thought, we said: 'Now nobody can tell us what to do!' Because Gregorio was dominated by his mother and was deathly afraid of her!"[33]

After Catalina gave birth in 1922 to Gregorio's only child, Catalinita, Gregorio left María. In 1924, his theater company performed in Barcelona for the season. Despite the situation and the distance, the relationship between Gregorio and María remained cordial: she continued to write plays and essays that Gregorio continued to perform and publish under his name.

IX   Theater Tour of America

In 1925, the Martínez Sierra Theater Company set out on an extended tour of Europe and America. Unfortunately, until the day the boat sailed no one knew if Catalina could leave the country. According to Spanish law, she needed her husband's consent for such a trip, and her legal husband, Ricardo Vargas — perhaps to spite her for real or imaginary ills he suffered over the years — refused to authorize the departure. Finally, on the day of the sailing, a legal separation was effected that allowed Catalina to travel.

The Martínez Sierra Company performed abroad under the title of Teatro de arte español (Spanish Art Theater). Included in the tour repertory were works characteristic of the Eslava days: the curious mixture of plays by Shakespeare, Shaw, Ibsen, and Martínez Sierra. Catalina Bárcena, of course, starred in these plays in London, Paris, Brussels, Berlin, and other European cities, as well as in the major theater capitals of North and South America. This very successful five-year tour would last until 1930 and included performances in Spain only in 1929.

In 1927, *Cradle Song* was performed in New York to very successful reviews, and Eva Le Gallienne subsequently incorporated the play into her repertory. *Cradle Song* became, in fact, the play she most often performed. *Autumn Spring* was also performed in New York, but reviews of this work were less enthusiastic. In 1929, Gregorio and Catalina returned to Madrid to open two new plays written by María: *La hora del diablo* (*The Devil's Hour*) and *Triángulo* (*Triangle*).

During the years of Gregorio's absence, María divided her time between Madrid and a small house she bought in Nice, France to escape from the cold winters. In addition to writing and mailing plays to Gregorio during this period, she became increasingly involved in the Socialist and feminist movements. In 1930, she was elected first president of the Asociación feminina de educación cívica (Women's Alliance for Civic Education). The goals of this organization of approximately fifteen hundred women from all strata of society were to educate women and men for the challenges of the modern world. The club provided a center where its members could congregate informally to exchange ideas and regularly hear lectures on a variety of cultural and practical topics. Rather than decorate its halls with elaborate tapestry, as was the custom for organizations in those days, this center prided itself on providing a library for members from the modest dues of two pesetas a month.

During Gregorio's long absence while on tour, María had been dependent on money he sent her, perhaps haphazardly, from various parts of the world. In 1930, Gregorio agreed to assign the royalties on all their works produced outside of Spain directly, legally, and exclusively to her. The new arrangement gave her a certain independence and sense of dignity that she could not have enjoyed before. At the time of the legal agreement, Gregorio cautioned María good-naturedly — but a trifle plaintively — not to succumb to bourgeois complacency now that she was living on the profits of past labors.[34]

X *Hollywood*

In 1931, at the peak of their prestige, Catalina and Gregorio were courted by the rapidly expanding film industry. Fearing that the theater would eventually succumb to motion pictures, they decided to accept contracts with Metro-Goldwyn-Mayer in Hollywood. In addition to assisting in the preparation of various movies for distribution to Spanish-speaking countries, Gregorio would supervise the film versions of *Mama* and *Autumn Spring* starring Catalina Bárcena.

Letters reveal that Gregorio adjusted easily to the climate, the landscape and the life-style of California. While he complained occasionally about the high cost of living, he assured María that the excellent products and accommodations were worth the money paid. He liked Americans, whom he found naive and genuine but rather uncultured. Although he respected the hard work and the technical competence of his co-workers in the film industry, he was bothered by animosity between the Spanish and the Latin American factions. His close friends during this period were José López Rubio, Enrique Jardiel Poncela and Edgar Neville, all of whom

would return to Spain to become major playwrights and active contributors to the Spanish film industry. The theater of all three was
affected and enriched by contacts with American film techniques.

Although Martínez Sierra was under contract to Metro-
Goldwyn-Mayer, he submitted stories for films on a freelance basis
to other studios. Urging María to send him all ideas she could think
of for this purpose, he wrote, "I want you to send me all the plots
that occur to you, good or bad. Forget the theater. Don't worry
about originality or shading. Since the movies are for everyone, they
[studios] prefer just rudimentary themes. They can be melodramas,
sentimental comedies, farces. The more action, the better. I think it
is worth our while to do this because we can live very well from this
activity with very little effort. But we have to think up many [plots]
in hopes that some will be bought. Don't fail to do it."[35] Similarly, in
several letters from Hollywood, Gregorio worried about María sending *Sortilegio* (*Spell*), a play he hoped to perform in the United
States and sell to a film studio. This script about a woman married to
a homosexual was apparently lost in the mails between Madrid and
Hollywood. It was performed in 1930 and 1942, but only in Buenos
Aires. As usual, Catalina Bárcena played the lead role.

In 1933, Paramount Pictures made a major production of *Cradle
Song*. The international star Dorothea Weick played the most maternal of the nuns, Sister Juana, and Evelyn Venable was Teresa,
the orphan reared by virginal mothers. Reviews uniformly praised
the sensitivity of the stars and the beauty of the photography as they
welcomed *Cradle Song* to the charmed circle of filmed masterpieces
of modern international drama. Meanwhile, María was campaigning
vigorously in 1933 for a seat in the Republic's Cortes (representative
legislative body). Sponsored by the Socialist Party of Granada,
María had been nominated by Granada's Socialist leader and Spain's
Minister of Education, Fernando de los Ríos (García Lorca's professor and close friend). On campaign trips through Granada, María
was depressed by the poverty, illiteracy, and the large numbers of
children borne by the women in this area.[36] Although she was especially interested in reaching women and involving them actively in
government (particularly in educational and cultural affairs), she
sought the support of men as well. In reference to having previously
beamed her message almost exclusively to women (in the feminist
essays and in the Feminine Alliance activities in Madrid), she
mused: "This time I'm not Isis speaking to Eves, but Eve trying to

convince some rather recalcitrant Adams."[37] María was successful in the election and represented Granada in the Republican government until the eruption of civil war in 1936.

XI *Exile*

After spending several lucrative years in Hollywood, Gregorio decided in 1935 to return to Spain. With the considerable money acquired in Hollywood, he planned to buy a theater in Madrid to continue in the art theater tradition he found so successful at the Eslava Theater and on tour. He and Catalina also planned to make a Spanish film of *Cradle Song* which Gregorio would direct and in which Catalina would star. The infant Spanish film industry, however, was not nearly as well organized or efficient as its American counterpart. Although Gregorio and Catalina signed contracts for *Cradle Song*, filming was delayed, and the outbreak of the Spanish Civil War in July of 1936 put an end to the project. Gregorio and Catalina, in Barcelona as the war started, decided quickly to accept the offer of an Argentine film company to produce *Cradle Song* and embarked for Buenos Aires.

At the beginning of the Spanish Civil War, the Republic sent María to Switzerland as commercial attaché, but she soon went to her cottage in Nice where she remained in exile after the Republic lost the war in 1939. However, the war did not end for María in 1939. The Germans occupied her house during the Second World War, and later she was forced to sell her property because she needed money.

Although after 1936 Gregorio mailed María packages of clothes, shoes, and food from Buenos Aires, he sent no money. In accordance with the agreement of 1930, María received certain royalties directly, while Gregorio collected others.

In Buenos Aires, Gregorio worked with theater and films. During the Second World War, he and Catalina lived comfortably but they were not happy: Gregorio because he was becoming increasingly inactive professionally, and Catalina because of a progressive hearing loss that had troubled her for years. Then, in 1947, Gregorio became alarmed about an abdominal condition stubbornly resistant to treatment. Perhaps suspecting the gravity of his illness, he decided to return to Madrid to consult with Spanish doctors. He also wanted to see his beloved Madrid again, of course. María, more stubborn and much more committed politically, refused, as did many exiles, to return to Spain as long as the Franco régime endured. In a last-minute effort to cling to life after returning to Madrid in 1947, Gregorio made plans for organizing a new theater company. Catalina, in her mid-fifties by then and almost totally deaf, would, of course, be his star.[38] Two weeks after his arrival, however, he died of abdominal cancer. In Nice, María heard the news of her husband's death via a British radio broadcast.

After Gregorio's death, María seemed inspired to write again. Did she feel that Gregorio's spirit, unencumbered by his body, would now return to her? Suggesting that such was the case, she dedicated her book *Gregorio and I* to "that Shadow that may have come — as he did so often when he had a body and eyes — to bend over my shoulder to see what I was writing," and in the book she wrote: "Do I dream that I am accompanied? What does it matter? When they are over, a reality and a dream leave an identical imprint on the spirit: a memory."[39]

After selling her property in France, María, at seventy-five years of age, set sail in 1950 for New York, taking with her several stories, dramatic sketches, scenarios, and plays she had written after Gregorio's death. The first of these plays, *Es así (That's the Way It Is)*, was performed by an amateur group at the University of Arizona in Tempe. After seeing the latter production, she continued on to Hollywood in hopes of meeting Walt Disney and selling him some of her stories. María, unaccustomed to standard practices of public relations that include generous doses of adulation and waiting, became discouraged and left for Mexico. She spent several months there in 1953 and published *Gregorio and I*. Because the climate of Mexico was not good for her health, she left for Argentina, where at seventy-eight she would make new friends and continue to work. In Buenos Aires, María told a reporter: "I need to work. That's the only way I really feel that I exist."[40]

Because María had been unsuccessful in contacting Walt Disney while in Hollywood, her American translator, Collice Portnoff, delivered several of María's stories to the Disney studio. The scripts were held for two months then politely returned. Subsequently Disney's *Lady and the Tramp*, bearing a striking similarity to a scenario María offered the studio, was filmed. María's story, published in *Voyages of a Water Drop* (1954), is entitled "Merlin and Viviana or the Selfish Cat and the Silly Dog."

In Buenos Aires María lived in a small hotel (the Deauville) and wrote several books as well as numerous articles and stories for *La Prensa* (*The Press*) and other Argentine journals. But her health degenerated, and she eventually left her Buenos Aires hotel to enter a rest home. In addition to frequent visits by her many friends, a consolation of her last years was a return to religion. In a final interview at ninety-nine years of age, María was asked if she still lacked faith in the Catholic religion as in her feminist-Socialist period of the 1930's. Becoming suddenly grave, María replied: "No. Some time ago, I returned to faith with the same sincerity and the same firmness with which I rejected it. I would not be able to live without the support of a religious belief. In my hours of anguish, before, now and always, the words 'my God' would come from the bottom of my soul, which means that whether I was a believer or not, I carried God within me, and into His hands I deliver myself in the final days of my life. I lost faith in everyone and in everything except in Him and He is now my great and only consolation."[41] In June of 1974, she died quietly in the San Camilo Sanitarium.

CHAPTER 2

The Literary Partnership: Exploitation, Collaboration, or Maternal Charity?

SINCE the Greek poet Sappho, who wrote lyric verse in the sixth century before Christ, there have been numerous other women poets, novelists, short story writers, and essayists. Theater, however, has remained singularly impenetrable to women, notably absent the world over from theatrical composition. Among women writing in Spanish prior to the nineteenth century, one can point only to the drama of Sister Juana Inés de la Cruz, hardly best remembered for her theatrical works. In the nineteenth and twentieth centuries, some Spanish women (i.e., Fernán Caballero, Gertrudis Gómez de Avellenada, Emilia Pardo Bazán, Concha Espina, Julia Maura, Pilar Encisco, Ana Diosdado) have composed for the stage but with relatively little success. Although María Martínez Sierra kept her identity hidden behind the name of her husband and has formal credit only in the case of foreign performances and translations (and only as joint author), her "secret" is widely known in Spanish theater circles. Precisely because women have not been successful playwrights (whether they used their own names or not) and were frequently ridiculed if they attempted to storm the barricades of that male-dominated bastion, dramaturgy, it is important to recognize María's achievement, for her plays were extraordinarily successful.

Because the bare facts of the literary partnership seem contradictory and prompt more questions than they answer, it is helpful to provide a historical and psychological framework within which evidence for María's authorship may be seen more clearly. In addition to reviewing what major critics have written concerning the literary collaboration, I will include several published statements made by Gregorio and María on the subject, speculate about María's motivations for concealing the extent of her participation, and probe the

40

perplexing enigmas of the María-Gregorio-Catalina (Bárcena) triangle. I am attempting, of course, to bring into focus the personalities of all three, but particularly of that formerly shadowy but remarkable figure: María Martínez Sierra. To provide detail to fill in outlines established by fact, I will also note pertinent impressions of theater people now in their seventies, eighties and nineties who worked closely with the principal characters of this real-life dramatic story. Since these surviving authors, actors, and artists were active witnesses to the Spanish stage from 1910 to 1930, it is important to record their recollections. Their opinions, subjective and ephemeral though they may be, provide a vital link with the past and bring personalities and motivations into meaningful — perhaps poignant — relief.

I *Speculation on the Collaboration*

The separation of what Gregorio suggested, wrote, and polished as opposed to what María suggested, wrote, and polished has long been a subject of speculation among theater spectators, professionals, critics, and friends. Those (principally spectators) who believe that María merely provided the feminine insights for Gregorio's woman-oriented theater are at one end of the spectrum. Occupying a middle ground are those, largely critics, who claim that María created the feminine characterizations and wrote the feminine dialogue as well. Finally, there are many — and these tend to be theater professionals — who feel certain that María authored singlehandedly most if not all of the works. All three groups attribute to María (but in varying degrees) plays which portray religious life, particularly that of the convents, in a humanized and realistic way: *Canción de cuna (Cradle Song); El reino de Dios (The Kingdom of God); Lirio entre espinas (Lily among Thorns); Los pastores (The Shepherds); Navidad (Holy Night)*. In these particular works, nuns are simply women with all the limitations, imperfections, and frustrations inherent in their humanity rather than idealized, mystical creatures romantically floating along moonlit, Romanesque galleries. María's stay with her sister, a nun in the *casa de misericordia* in León, to prepare for what was to become her favorite work, *The Kingdom of God*, provided additional incentive for this widely-held attribution to her of the convent plays.[1]

II *The Triangular Collaboration of
Gregorio, María, and Catalina*

About 1907, Gregorio, the aspiring playwright, was making the
rounds of various theaters and met Catalina Bárcena, a young ingenue actress, who in time would dominate his amorous as well as
his theatrical life. Gregorio, early recognizing Catalina's considerable gifts, provided the direction she needed, becoming over the
years a mentor-svengali, making her the leading Spanish actress of
the day. In 1917, he and Catalina formed their own theater company
with Gregorio as artistic director and Catalina as lead actress.

Co-workers recall that Catalina was the most extraordinary and
most intuitive performer they had ever known, and that she was
especially admired for her beautiful and melodious stage voice. Because of a progressive hearing loss that began early in life, however,
Catalina tended to speak too loud in private conversations and de-
manded that others reply in tones that she could understand.
Catalina, the incarnation of the many charming, intelligent, cul-
tured, independent, strong yet thoroughly feminine heroines of the
works of Martínez Sierra, was, say some, totally dependent on Gregorio in minor as well as major matters. She took direction only from
him and sought his advice even about what she should wear or eat
for lunch. Ironically, the public images of both Catalina and María
contrast with their private personalities as recalled by friends.
María, one of Spain's most active early feminists, was personally
soft-spoken, sweet, and totally lacking in aggressive tendencies. She
consistently avoided attracting attention to herself by sitting in the
back rows at rehearsals and by communicating her suggestions to
Gregorio privately.

There is no indication that María ever confronted Gregorio angrily regarding Catalina. She never confided her anxiety, if she felt
it, to her family or to members of the theater company.[2] Catalina,
on the other hand, was intensely jealous of María, and when she
bore Gregorio's daughter, Catalinita, in 1922, she threatened to
stop acting if Gregorio did not live with her rather than María. Had
María threatened to stop writing if Gregorio left her, a most interesting crisis would have developed. Obviously not averse to
using people through collaborations, Gregorio probably would have
opted for the woman who helped him most. In the opinion of

friends, "success" was Gregorio's politics and his religion. Because María created no such crisis, however, Gregorio was able to continue to have his cake and eat it too: he lived with Catalina and their daughter while María continued to write for him.

Despite the new living arrangements, Gregorio continued to see María quite regularly. He usually spent one day a week with her to discuss professional matters. María, proud of her many domestic accomplishments, would personally prepare lunch, and then — curiously enough, without friction — Gregorio would return to Catalina.[3]

In 1924, Gregorio relinquished directorship of the Eslava to spend a year with his theater company at Barcelona's Novedades Theater, and the following year, he and Catalina took the company on a tour of Europe and America that was to last five years. Correspondence reveals that the literary association with María continued despite the separation.

Gregorio needed — and indeed managed to be "married" to — two women of enormously different personalities.[4] María was the calm, independent, supportive, intellectually compatible, maternally indulgent mate, while Catalina was the beautiful, challenging, unsettling, demanding, dependent one. According to an actor who traveled with the company for years, Gregorio and Catalina quarreled constantly, mostly about Gregorio's refusal to separate — physically at first, then legally — from María. This same source believes that María was the woman Gregorio loved most; his justification was that between these two women, "there was no comparison." He may, however, have been projecting his own tastes on Gregorio.

Gregorio's letters to María during the separation reveal his continuing need for the literary wife; apparently he had less and less time to write. Indeed, Gregorio's contribution to literary and dramatic work after 1924 was very likely limited to editorial suggestions. From Barcelona he urged María to complete the stage version of their novel *Torre de marfil (Ivory Tower)* as soon as possible, for he desperately needed a new play to perform. Actors began rehearsals as soon as the first act arrived and nervously awaited subsequent installments. As María's scripts were delivered, Gregorio, apparently overjoyed, sent her such encouraging telegrams as: "Wonderful first act"; "Second act perfect."[5] *Mujer (Woman)* and

Cada uno y su vida (To Each His Own), probably the work of María, were also successfully performed in 1924 and starred, of course, Catalina Bárcena.[6]

While no correspondence between Gregorio and Catalina is available, the letters between Gregorio and María are serene and quietly affectionate. In approximately one hundred fifty letters that span twenty-five years (concentrated between 1915 and 1930), Gregorio mentions Catalina to María only twice, and then in reference to a performance, calling her on both occasions "La Bárcena." María never mentions Catalina in the few letters to Gregorio that I have seen. (Most of these were, of course, in the possession of Gregorio). His letters suggest that Catalina was a subject they never broached.

Ironically enough, without the separation and the consequent need for correspondence, it is likely that proof of María's writing — and indeed her exclusive authorship in the case of several works — would never have come to light. Perhaps too, Gregorio might have collaborated more actively with María had they continued living together. One wonders, however, about María's motives in preserving letters that substantiate her authorship. Perhaps she kept them for sentimental reasons, for she never used them, even after Gregorio's death and the subsequent revelation of a will that assigned the royalties of certain works to Catalinita, his daughter. Had María really wanted to conceal her extensive contribution, she could have destroyed the letters; and had she really wanted to establish her authorship — and hence ownership — of the works, she could have produced irrefutable court evidence in her favor. She neither destroyed the letters nor used them, although she never denied having collaborated with Gregorio. Her position (based, perhaps, on her deep desire) was that Gregorio had been her partner in everything and that they had written all the works together. María's stubborn, almost pathological insistence that all work was accomplished with Gregorio may have been an expression of her own need to believe it — a way, indeed, of denying the painful reality of separation.

Even in her partially autobiographical work, *Gregorio and I* (1953), when María had the perfect opportunity to clarify her contribution, she sidestepped the nature of her role in over one hundred original works (some unpublished) and the many translations from French, Italian, English, and Catalan that bear the signature of Gregorio Martínez Sierra. In *Gregorio and I* she writes of the collaboration in a very general way as though everyone knew about it. She refers to the fruit of their endeavors as "our children," and focuses characteristically on the happy moments of their literary partnership. Oddly enough, she includes in this partnership even the sixteen years (1931–1947) of Gregorio's life in which he and Catalina were living in Hollywood or Buenos Aires, while she remained in Madrid and Nice.

III *Published References to the Collaboration*

Published references of literary historians, critics, and journalists to the collaboration of Gregorio and María tend to be guarded and vague. Although there have been some bold exceptions to this rule, no one has offered supporting documentation. The English critic, dramatist, director, and actor H. Granville-Barker, in an introduction to John Garret Underhill's two-volume translation of Martínez Sierra's theater, writes: "María Martínez Sierra, an accomplished writer and one of the most brilliant women in Spain, has brought to her husband a store of feminine lore and intuition through a long series of collaborations whose precise nature and scope the most patient criticism could not hope to disclose."[7]

The McGraw-Hill Encyclopedia of Works of Drama a little more boldly but no more specifically affirms: "All works bearing the name of Gregorio Martínez Sierra are acknowledged to be the joint efforts of husband and wife."[8] Meanwhile, Gonzalo Torrente Ballester, rather cautiously conservative about the collaboration, skirts the issue after faulting Gregorio for his lack of virility: "When we deal with Martínez Sierra and this problem [virility], we must mention the possible collaboration of his wife in his dramatic works."[9] In *A New History of Spanish Literature*, Richard E. Chandler and Kessel Schwartz write of Martínez Sierra: "His wife, María de la O Lejárraga, an ardent feminist, collaborated with him in many of his dramas, and it has been said that his penetrating feminine psychology may be due in part to her assistance."[10] Similarly, Angel Lázaro Carreter and E. Correa Calderón conclude several paragraphs dedicated to Martínez Sierra in this fashion: "The abundance of women characters and feminine points of view have led people to think that he relied on the collaboration of his wife, María de la O Lejárraga."[11]

In his *Historia de la literatura española: Siglo veinte*, B. B. Brown cautiously suggests: "A predominance of feminine characters in the theater of Martínez Sierra, a general preoccupation with affirming the dignity of Spanish mothers and a gentle adhesion to the feminist cause contributed to the general belief that some of his works were, in reality, written by his wife."[12] Even in their *Brief Survey of Spanish Literature*, Nicholson Adams and John Keller mention the possible collaboration of María: "In some plays, one feels the influence of Maeterlinck, and perhaps the participation of his gifted wife, María de la O Lejárraga."[13] Less timid is the passage in *Artículos de crítica teatral: El teatro español de 1914 a 1936*, wherein Enrique Diez-Canedo states that Gregorio Martínez Sierra has, "with the undeclared collaboration of his wife, María de la O Lejárraga, produced many works brimming with a tenderness and optimism which later evolved into a sense of social apostolacy."[14] Francisco Ruiz Ramón in his *Historia del teatro español: Siglo veinte* quotes the above statement of Diez-Canedo without additional comment on the question of authorship.[15]

Dealing with the matter in a lengthy section of his monumental fourteen-volume study of the Spanish language and literature, Julio Cejador y Frauca announces positively, but without supporting evidence, that María and Gregorio are the "literary Martínez Sierra" and that their works bear Gregorio's name only because such was María's wish.[16] In addition, Cejador calls the literary personality of Martínez Sierra: "an admirable and rarely seen combination of masculine and feminine virtues that make for truly human art; the work of two persons, man and woman, in which the feminine tone in manner, effects, and form seem to predominate and provide its special trademark" (178). After praising Martínez Sierra for being a pioneer in effectively utilizing stasis, detail, tenderness, and compassion in his dramatic art, Cejador suggests that these innovations are the contribution of María rather than Gregorio and adds: "Perhaps we have had an excess of men writers when what we needed was women writers, for women more than men appreciate these delicate shadings of the human heart. The work of Martínez Sierra, the product of a man and a woman, could — and perhaps necessarily had to — be this kind of work" (182). In discussing the cameo quality of *Cradle Song*, Cejador continues to laud Martínez Sierra's sensitivity for the more delicate emotions and again attributes this important quality to the contribution of María: "These small details are not customarily important to the purely masculine writer; but the woman hidden behind the name of her husband Martínez Sierra had to see them and feel them. Is this effeminate writing, then? No, it is simply human. The complete human, man and woman, provides the dramatic temperament that we have here and that we have needed for a long time in the theater" (183).

Demonstrating not only much admiration for the work signed by Martínez Sierra, but for María as a person, Cejador continues:

Despite María's great and sincere modesty, one must make clear that she is an extraordinary woman. She continues to practice her profession as a teacher, she is very much the lady of her house, and she avoids attracting public attention to herself. To speak of her writing, of the triumphs of her works, and of the praise that newspapers and magazines accord her is simply to annoy her and put her in a bad humor. It is not that she scorns glory or finds praise unpleasant, for such would be rather unnatural and go against human nature, but the inconsequential criticism and the glorification that characterize the judgments of most of the critics have made her abhor all attention to her work, and she doesn't want them [critics] to speak of her. It is, then, an extraordinary modesty that denies the rare talent she cannot help but be aware of; a talent much larger and more philosophical than that possessed by the run-of-the-mill women writers who go to great lengths to be talked about and who frequent literary circles uninvited. Let's leave doña María to her reserve and, as she wishes, let's call Martínez Sierra the author of the work in which she has participated as much or more than her husband. "Everything is his," she says, "and I don't have to figure at all." But I and the rest of Gregorio's friends are convinced to the contrary, and the truth has its rights. (185–86)

Making a reference to Cejador's position, Luciano García Lorenzo writes in 1975: "And if Martínez Sierra counted on Catalina Bárcena to present his spectacles, we must necessarily point to his wife, María de la O Lejárraga, as we discuss his work as a dramatist. How much did the wife collaborate in the composition of the works? Was she simply a help — as some claim — or should the theater of Martínez Sierra also bear the signature of María, a position Cejador favored?"[17]

Conversely, Aubrey F. G. Bell, in *Contemporary Spanish Literature,* is reticent about attributing to María the feminine characterizations:

The collaboration of Don Gregorio Martínez Sierra and of his wife, Doña María Lejárraga, is as closely interwoven as that of the brothers Álvarez

Quintero in their *sainetes*. The sympathetic interest in the development of the female characters need by no means be the mark of a woman's hand, and a certain feminine strain might be characteristic of a Modernist writer; but the feminist outlook in the *Sueño de una noche de Agosto* [sic], *La mujer del Héroe* [sic], *Pobrecito Juan* and other plays no doubt represents the well-known feminist views of Doña María Lejárraga, to whom likewise may be ascribed something of the delicacy of the craftsmanship."[18]

Ricardo Gullón, with the assurance that careful documentation and thorough familiarity of the individuals involved provides, writes the following in the course of his introductory study to *Relaciones amistosas y literarias entre Juan Ramón Jiménez y los Martínez Sierra:*

It is impossible to write the history of Spanish literary Modernism without taking into account the person and the work of Gregorio Martínez Sierra and with him, the person and work of his wife and collaborator, María de la O Lejárraga García. . . . From 1898, the year his first book was published, until 1907, he published, assisted by his tireless wife, no less than twenty-two works. . . . When I speak of the works of Gregorio Martínez Sierra, I refer to those signed by him and written with his wife. . . . Later they decided to adopt the name "Gregorio Martínez Sierra" to designate the work of both. The wife spent most of her time writing and "researching" — while the husband, irresistibly drawn to theatrical direction and the literary life, took care of those necessary tasks that we might designate public relations for the G.M.S. Corporation. . . . In April of 1903, *Helios*, the best Modernist journal, begins publication. Among its editor-collaborators figured Juan Ramón Jiménez and G. Martínez Sierra — that is to say María and Gregorio — , Pedro González Blanco, Ramón Pérez de Ayala and Carlos Navarro Lamarca. And the figure of María, silent and shadowy collaborator, is exceptional for her time and place.[19]

The most positive stand among the scholarly critics was taken by Pedro González Blanco, brother of Andrés and Edmundo. All three brothers, creative writers as well as critics, were close personal friends of Gregorio and María. They, with Juan Ramón Jiménez, Ramón Pérez de Ayala, Jacinto Benavente, José Ortega y Gasset (under the pseudonym of Rubín de Cendoya), the Machado brothers, and other literary figures, collaborated with the Martínez Sierras on one or more of the Modernist journals (*Modern Life, The Sun, Renaissance*) which the couple founded between 1901 and

1907. Of the commentators in print, it is Pedro González Blanco who writes with most conviction. While his general attribution of everything to María may be excessive, his itemized credits seem quite reasonable:

But is there certainty about that collaboration? Absolutely not. Gregorio Martínez Sierra never wrote anything that circulates under his name, whether it be novel, essay, poetry, or theater. That is something that Juan Ramón Jiménez, Ramón Pérez de Ayala and I know well. That is something that Usandizada knew extremely well: the libretto for *Las golondrinas* [*The Swallows*] is by María —; Turina knew it — the libretto for *Margot* is by María —; Falla knew it — the directions for the ballets for *El sombrero de tres picos* [*The Three-Cornered Hat*] and *El amor brujo* [*Love's Sorcery*] are by María —; that is something that Marquina knew well — *El pavo real* [*The Peacock*] was written by María and put into verse by Eduardo; Arniches knew it — two acts of *La chica del gato* [*The Girl with the Cat*] are María's — etc. But those who knew it best were the actors who were always nervous when they left Madrid and especially when they were traveling around America: "The third act that Doña María has to send hasn't arrived yet, and we'll have to suspend the rehearsals." "I hear there's a cable from Doña María saying that she has mailed the play," etc.[20]

Although many literary critics deal with Martínez Sierra without reference to a collaboration with María, the silence of Federico Carlos Sainz de Robles and Andrés Goldsborough Serrat on this subject deserves some attention. Sainz de Robles, in the biographical and critical introductions to three volumes of Martínez Sierra's works *(Teatro, Novela,* and *Ensayos)*, deals at some length with the accusations of critics regarding the feminine overtones of the author's works.[21] While he quotes Cejador, thereby demonstrating familiarity with the likelihood of María's participation, he fails to mention her at all, even as Gregorio's wife. He does, however, include praise of Catalina Bárcena as an artistic collaborator of the dramatist.[22]

Andrés Goldsborough Serrat mentions María only once in an entire book on Martínez Sierra. In an effort, perhaps, not to offend Catalina Bárcena — whom he thanks profusely in the Preface and mentions frequently in the text — he makes note of María only in these terms: "At twenty years of age, he married unexpectedly. His family was quite surprised. They knew the girl because they had been sweethearts for a year, but such a hasty decision was unexpected. The girl's name was María de la O Lejárraga, and she was a language teacher in a girls' school where she taught French, English, and Russian. But the marriage did not cut short the career of Martínez Sierra as many people expected."[23]

The journalist-critics were generally more fearless and outspoken in support of María. In a newspaper article, Peón de Brega writes: "Doña María, at the side of Martínez Sierra, collaborates with him and in reality writes the plays that circulate in print under the latter's name. . . . Without diminishing the personality of either of them, we can affirm that the writer was María and the theatrical artisan was Gregorio, who conceived the theatrical situations."[24] Letters from Gregorio speaking of plot lines and stories that he planned to send her suggest that such was his contribution, in the later years, at least. Arturo de Romay also supports María's authorship: "María Lejárraga de Martínez Sierra has in her possession fifty literary and theatrical works, thought out, discussed, and planned with Gregorio her husband, and all, except one, written by her alone. Of these works the novel *You Are Peace* and the plays *The Kingdom of God, Don Juan of Spain*, and *Cradle Song* would be sufficient to ensure a reputation."[25]

Indalecio Prieto makes interesting evaluations of Catalina Bárcena and María Martínez Sierra before attributing four-fifths of the works to María:

Catalina Bárcena, as frequently happens with actresses who on stage play ingenue roles, became the *femme fatale*, destroying a happy marriage. But María Lejárraga never — not even after confirming the infidelity — ceased to attribute to Gregorio everything she wrote. More than four-fifths of the literary production attributed to Gregorio Martínez Sierra should be credited exclusively to María Lejárraga, who continued calling herself María Martínez Sierra; she neither complained nor protested until, helpless and exiled, she sought legal aid, because the plays that she and only she wrote (Gregorio devoted his energies to theatrical direction and production as stage director and theatrical impresario) continue to be performed in Spain and abroad, especially *Cradle Song*, which, translated into several languages, has toured the world in triumph.[26]

In a newspaper article published in Spain on the occasion of the televised version of *Cradle Song* in New York, W. K. Mayo writes the following: "What American admirers of Martínez Sierra do not know is that when Martínez Sierra separated from his wife, María de la O Lejárraga, he stopped writing. . . . What has been said, and apparently with good reason, is that the author of the literary and theatrical works of Martínez Sierra was his wife."[27] And, apparently referring to a previously published article or comment, Joaquín Alcaraz, in a letter to the editor of *Excelsiór* (a Mexican newspaper), writes: "I want to support what Ceferino Avecilla very correctly says regarding María Lejárraga de Martínez Sierra. I was the prompter in Martínez Sierra's theatrical company for more than ten years, and I toured North and South America with him. We were always waiting for an act — or acts — from María. In the company, we all knew that Gregorio didn't write, not even letters to his family. We were always on tenterhooks waiting for María to send original plays or translations. At times, we even had to cancel rehearsals to wait for what María was sending."[28]

IV   *Gregorio and María on the Collaboration*

Although one might suspect Gregorio of wanting María to remain anonymous in order to claim all the credit for their writing, such apparently was not the case. In correspondence with her family (1939–1969), María mentions several times that Gregorio encouraged her to sign the works as co-author. María acknowledges his position in a paragraph preliminary to a list of her translations into Spanish. She also mentions the legal document Gregorio prepared in 1930 declaring her his collaborator on all works. Writing of herself in the third person, María offers this rather pathetic explanation: "She never signed them [the works] because she didn't want to — in spite of Martínez Sierra's constant desire that she do so — for a variety of romantic reasons and whims. Since Gregorio, her collaborator, has died, she signs what she writes because she has no choice if she is to collect royalties. In the face of death, romanticism has no place."[29] Although during their life together, many personal friends were aware of María's extensive writing, she kept details of the collaboration to herself. Gregorio would speak proudly of her work when occasions presented themselves, however, even when he knew his comments would be published. Responding, for example, to an American Hispanist's inquiry about the rumor of collaboration, Gregorio made this statement: "Yes, sir, my wife contributes to my literary work. She is my collaborator and has more talent than I do. It is more than that; while I struggled, I didn't want to say anything; but now we have succeeded and I want it to be known, and there is nothing that makes me prouder than for people to say that my wife has talent. My wife and I love each other so much and we get along so well that in this case one can really say that we are one person; in the many disappointments that I have had, the first to bolster my spirits has been my wife."[30] This is the only published pronouncement by Gregorio I have seen on the collaboration, the nature of which he too leaves quite open.

Although married Spanish women traditionally retain their maiden names, María felt after marriage that Martínez Sierra was her name. A cosmopolitan woman, an inveterate traveler and a student of English, María held great fondness and respect for England. She may have considered this country more enlightened about women and hence adopted its system for her name. (In 1900, however, when she adopted her husband's name, she had not yet demonstrated any interest in feminism.) Never after marriage, not even after the separation from him and the death of Gregorio, did María use the name Lejárraga — or, as would have been normal and customary, the variants de (of) Martínez Sierra or Viuda de (Widow of) Martínez Sierra. Having adopted Martínez Sierra as her name and symbol of her oneness with Gregorio, she wrote in 1953 of the joy she felt at seeing it in print (after 1900): "our name, 'Gregorio Martínez Sierra,' voluntarily adopted as the symbol of our youthful joy. . . ."[31]

In Gregorio and I, María gives several reasons for not signing her own name to the works. Among others, she cites a fit of temper caused by the family's casual reception of her first book, the only one, in fact, which would ever bear the name "María de la O Lejárraga":

We managed to publish Labor's Poem and Short Stories in secret, pooling our meager savings. Since I was a teacher, I signed the stories because they were for children, while he, already recognized as a poet, signed the poem. On the very day of their publication, we took them to our respective homes. At my collaborator's house, a book! It was almost a miracle, and the first-born was received with all honors: surprise, rejoicing, family pride. I believe that they even uncorked champagne for the celebration. In my house, where there were so many books, two more — even though the first-born signed one of them and the other the "little friend" that my parents and brothers and sisters already suspected would become my fiancé — didn't mean much. The event sparked neither enthusiasm nor celebration. In my pride as a new author, I had expected a better reception. I felt inside — the way I always do — a really terrible rage, and I swore up and down: "Never again will you see my name printed on the cover of a book!"[32] María's restrained and "interior" tantrum must have been, as she suggests, "terrible," for it lasted seventy-six years. It may also help explain her total rejection of the name Lejárraga. Continuing to muse about why she did not want her name to appear as author, María writes:

I decided that the children of our intellectual union would not carry other than the father's name. Another reason was that being a school teacher, that is, carrying out a public responsibility, I didn't want to sully the purity of my name with the doubtful fame that fell like the heretic's smock in those days over any "literary" woman, especially a novice. If it were just possible to be famous from the first book! Fame justifies everything. The third reason, perhaps the strongest one, was the romanticism of a woman in love. Married, young, and happy, I was seized by that pride and humility that dominate every woman when she truly loves a man. Because our works are the offspring of a legitimate marriage, with the father's name they have sufficient honor.[33]

In 1953 when María arrived in Buenos Aires, the city in which she would spend the remainder of her life, she made this statement: "Why didn't I sign my works with Gregorio? I had many reasons. I wanted to enjoy a sweet anonymity and a kind of spontaneous yielding to my husband, the head of the household. On the other hand, I was four years older than he. I had the impression that I would die first."[34]

Years later, in an article published on the occasion of her approaching ninetieth birthday, María reiterated her resentment of the family's lack of enthusiasm on the publication of her first book:

I didn't sign the works because when I was a girl I made an oath. I'll tell you about it: When we published our respective first books, Gregorio took his to his house and they gave a huge party with champagne and everything. In my house something different happened. Everyone lived reading and writing, and when I presented my book, nobody thought it was important. Everyone thought it was the most natural thing in the world . . . and gave it no thought. I threw a real tantrum on the inside (mind you, I only throw them on the inside); I felt so terrible that I swore to them: "You'll never see my name again on the cover of a book." And I kept that promise until Gregorio died. Now I sign my works, because if I don't sign, I don't collect, and if I don't collect, I don't eat.[35]

In the same article quoted above, María spoke rather freely on the subject of her collaboration with Gregorio. Early in the interview, she could have provided support for the faction that considers María responsible only for feminine characterizations and dialogue in the plays. Because of Gregorio's extensive business commitments, however, she confesses that she alone was writing in the later years: "Dramatic art requires criticism, a lot of criticism, and no matter how good a critic one is, there is no doubt that four eyes see more than two. Besides, men don't make good women, just as women authors don't make good men. At first, we both wrote, or whoever had more time. Finally, I did it alone because Gregorio was a businessman, a theatrical director, a founder of publishing houses. He was a man of enormous activity."[36] Gregorio's letters support her statement.

In another interview in Buenos Aires, María made a similar statement about the collaboration but was slightly more expansive. In answer to the question about who had written the works, she replied: "Whoever had more time. There was a period in which we both did. Gregorio had more time than I did at first. I worked as a teacher and besides had to take care of the house. Later on, things changed. Outside of literature, Gregorio had other things to do: he was director of the Eslava Theater and also managed Renacimiento, the publishing house that was the salvation of Spanish writers. Then I began to write most of our works. I never stopped counting on Gregorio's collaboration, however. He always thought up the best things. He had a very fertile imagination."[37]

Responding to an interviewer's question about who had written the feminist essays, *Cartas a las mujeres de España (Letters to the Women of Spain*, 1916), in a moment of unusual candor, María replied: "I wrote them in Cao Ferrat, Santiago Rusiñol's house in Sitges. . . ."[38] Later in the interview, in reference to the dramatic team of Joaquín and Serafín Álvarez Quintero, she may have tacitly defended the rather passive contribution of Gregorio in the later years: "I am sure that Joaquín, who had a wonderful sense of the comic, never wrote a line, but no one can say that they didn't compose the works together. They collaborated very closely."[39] Joaquín reportedly suggested situations and characters while Serafín did the actual writing. Correspondence suggests that María and Gregorio had a similar arrangement.

Realizing in 1973 that time was running out for consultation with María, I wrote her in a last-minute effort to unravel some of the knotty issues of the collaboration. María, then ninety-eight years old, troubled with arthritis and living in a Buenos Aires rest home, was unable to reply personally to correspondence. Antonio Sempere, a nephew-in-law, responded to my letter expressing his willingness to speak to María and relay responses to me. Among others, I asked the following questions: How was the work divided? Did she write, for example, the dialogue of the women characters while he wrote the speeches of the men? Did he write one act and she another? Or did they do everything together and at the same time? After consulting with María, Mr. Sempere responded: "The collaboration between husband and wife was complete. They did not divide their work into set areas, but, in accordance with inspiration and time, they would complete the works." In answer to a specific question about *The Kingdom of God*, the work most often attributed entirely to María, Sempere wrote: "Doña María does not recall the proportion of her influence in that work." Naturally I wondered if María was simply being stubborn or if old age had indeed taken its toll on her memory.

In the 1964 interview, María had admitted authoring the feminist essays. In answer to this question: "Did they write the feminist essays together?" the reply through Sempere was affirmative with some reservations: "Yes. Naturally Doña María was, for obvious reasons, much more feminist than Don Gregorio, who became interested in feminism through her." Although María clarified certain biographical points, she remained characteristically noncommittal on the literary collaboration. In response to another question that attempted to probe the nature and extent of the partnership came this tight-lipped yet concessive reply: "All the works were written in collaboration, but some almost exclusively by María. . . ."[40]

María's death in June of 1974 put an end to our correspondence. At that time, and lacking tangible proof, several newspapers again printed what had been rumored for years. Josefina Carabias in *Ya* wrote: "It was said that all the plays that Gregorio Martínez Sierra signed and performed had been written in reality by his wife, although they had been separated for some time."[41] José Prat, implying that María was the creative hand, ventured: "Gregorio was the great theatrical director and María was the anonymous and tireless writer. He doubtless was more skilled in poetry and she was more fertile in prose. In the case of the Quintero brothers, it is almost impossible to separate the work of one from the other. Perhaps a similar situation exists in the case of Gregorio Martínez Sierra. Brilliant in the theater and in conversation, he signed, while María in the silence of her home or hotel rooms wrote ceaselessly."[42] Ángel Lázaro, in *La Vanguardia*, called María the "inspiration of everything" as well as "author of some books and plays they both signed; partial author of some, and sole author of others."[43]

During the summer of María's death (1974), I spoke to several people in Madrid who might, I hoped, shed some light on the writing arrangement as well as on the human contradictions of Gregorio and María's relationship. I found lines tightly drawn between the María camp and the pro-Catalina faction: those who considered themselves friends of the latter hardly acknowledged the existence of María, while friends of María studiously avoided mention of Catalina. Although I consulted members of both factions in approximately equal proportions, I found myself drawn into the polemic also. The situation was so intriguing that one could hardly remain aloof from its compelling human drama.

Throughout her relationship with Gregorio, María, in words and actions, demonstrated an indulgent, forgiving, and maternal attitude. In an interview already quoted above, María exemplified these qualities as she gave this explanation of why only Gregorio's name appeared on the works:

Because we had made that agreement. But about the time of the war in Spain, I told him that I wanted my signature to appear because then I would receive royalties also. And that's the way it was. But Gregorio pulled a trick on me: instead of publishing the books with Gregorio and María Martínez Sierra, he put only the initials "G. and M." Martínez Sierra. Then, when I came to Buenos Aires, I found out that when a naive reader would ask him who "M." was, he would say it was his brother. Imagine such a thing! But I didn't get too angry because I always loved him very much.[44]

Hazarding a rare reference to Catalina (the only published one that I have seen), the interviewer rather boldly commented to María: "Despite the fact that Gregorio lived with Catalina Bárcena for many years, we understand that the relationship between you and him was never really interrupted." María, apparently unabashed, responded: "Never. We wrote each other frequently, we told each other the news, and besides, he continued needing me."[45] María obviously enjoyed having Gregorio need her — even if it was only to write plays for him — just as she must have enjoyed in some sense filling his need. When asked if she collected royalties on the works signed by her deceased husband, María made a candid and balanced reference to Catalina that agreed in substance with appraisals of friends as well as foes. María's comment seems strangely lacking in indignation: "Yes. I share them with a daughter of Catalina and Gregorio. He was so good, and at times, so naive! Catalina never liked me. I thought she was charming to look at, but that's all she had. But, as I tell you, she couldn't stand me."[46]

V *María's Credo: "Only the Serene Hours"*

Considering María's active personality and belief in women's rights, her passive — almost self-effacing — attitude seems contradictory. María was, however, a militant Pollyanna who forced herself to suppress unpleasantness. She wrote, for example, the three hundred fourteen-page book of her professional life with Gregorio without mentioning Catalina a single time, even though this actress was a major factor in their theatrical success. In the preface to this book, María expounds briefly on her optimistic philosophy of life as she explains the title of the foreword, "Horas serenas" ("The Serene Hours"): "One day, in some forgotten garden of the world, I saw a sand clock with this motto written in Latin: 'I point only to the serene hours.' *Nisi serenas*. This has always been my life's motto as well. Not a voluntary or chosen motto, but an instinctive one; it has been a lucky gift, a grace from God. *Nisi serenas*. I have instinctively known how to preserve in my memory only the serene hours. Whoever wants to recall and recount any others is unfortunate and miserable."[47] Then, in a curious interior monologue, she may allude to Catalina's absence in the book: "What materials do you keep, child, for building your treasure? Pure gold, the simple kernel. Everything else into the crematory oven of forgetfulness. Are you going to keep decay to corrode your existence? Rancid bitternesses to poison the air you breathe and that gives you life? Whom would you like to blackmail, preserving the memory of evil actions? Grudges? Toxins in the blood. What for? With what right? Forgiveness suggests that you have judged, and what kind of intolerable arrogance is that? You, a judge? Not even of yourself."[48]

While María outwardly took no notice of Catalina, friends recall that Catalina displayed moments of jealousy and temperament about María. She may well have resented Gregorio's Friday visits with María and the regular and affectionate — not passionate — correspondence he maintained with her while the theater company was on tour. And too, perhaps being serenely ignored by María was sufficient to infuriate an actress accustomed to attention.

Jaime Lejárraga, María's nephew and a director of Aguilar Publishing House in Madrid, was involved in plans after Gregorio's death for a new edition of the *Obras completas (Complete Works)*. Since Gregorio's will had left rights of some plays to María and rights of others to his daughter, Catalinita (and through her to Catalina, of course), both women had to agree on publication details. When Catalina learned that María planned to write the introduction to the contemplated edition, she withdrew permission and the project was abandoned.[49]

VI   *Literary Expressions of the Triangle*

If María, whatever her reasons, failed to take public note of Catalina, she may well have used material from the triangular relationship for plays composed after 1923. Correspondence indicates she alone wrote *Mujer (Woman,* 1923), *Torre de marfil (Ivory Tower,* 1924), *Seamos felices (Let's Be Happy,* 1929), *La hora del diablo (The Devil's Hour,* 1930), and *Triángulo (Triangle,* 1930) and that Gregorio's intervention was limited to suggestions or modifications for plot and character. Examination of these last five works also reveals that all, except *Let's Be Happy,* deal with a triangle involving two women competing for the love of one man.

A writer living close to Gregorio in Hollywood in 1930, when the script of *Triangle* appeared as though by magic, feels certain that Gregorio was writing nothing at the time and that María mailed the script to him. Letters substantiate his suspicion. This play *(Triangle)* in which a man must choose between a quiet, maternal, indulgent wife and a beautiful, demanding, unsettling one could have been an intellectualized version of the María-Gregorio-Catalina triangle. If María did write the play — and I accept the evidence that she did — she certainly provided a balanced, even good-natured, vision of the situation. In addition she gave the work a male focus, difficult, one would think, under the circumstances.

Faustino, the protagonist, believes that his first wife has died in a shipwreck and marries again. The fun and conflicts begin when the very alive and lively wife number one (who was rescued off the African coast by savages believing her to be a goddess) returns to resume the marriage. With only a hint of sadism along with her customary good humor, María allows Faustino to be torn between wives of very different qualities without favoring either. In a technique reminiscent of Pirandello's *Six Characters in Search of An Author*, the anguished Faustino ultimately finds a solution in autonomy. As though suddenly able to awaken from this nightmare, he realizes that he is merely a character in a play and leaps from the stage as the women pursue him.

Faustino joins the audience to become a spectator to the dilemma from which he has conveniently and effectively removed himself. Although they understand the trick he has played, they seem unable to follow him, remaining imprisoned in the confines of the work. At this point, the play is over. The triangle has ceased to exist, and each viewer must find his own solution to the problem of whether a man needs a spiritual wife or a physical one. The play ultimately says that Faustino — and by extension, Gregorio — needs diverse qualities in a spouse, and that at times one mate is insufficient to meet one's complex needs. In Faustino's case (as in Gregorio's), life would have been quite incomplete with only one of the women represented, for at times he needed the security and comfort of the mother-wife and at times he needed the stimulation of the temptress-wife. One would think that had María been upset by the real-life triangle, she would have created a melodrama — if not a tragedy — rather than a light-hearted comedy. Taking into account María's determined optimism and considerable good humor may lessen the contradictions inherent in attributing this play to her.

VII *Gregorio's Acknowledgment*

Having read that there existed a document signed by Gregorio formally acknowledging María's collaboration, I asked María's nephew, Jaime Lejárraga, if he knew anything about it. He promised to ask his sister Margarita, who had lived several years with María in France after the Spanish Civil War. At our next meeting, he brought not only the requested document, but pictures[50] and the interesting information that his sister possessed considerable correspondence between Gregorio and María. I was eager to see the letters, but for the moment was fascinated by the half page before me in Gregorio's small, stilted handwriting and signed by two witnesses, Enrique Ucelay and Eusebio La Gorbea.[51] It stated: "I declare for legal purposes that all my works are written in collaboration with my wife, Doña María de la O Lejárraga y García, and to bind this statement, I affix my signature in Madrid on the fourteenth of April, 1930."[52]

Several days later, I visited Margarita Lejárraga, a devoted niece of María, who kept the complete works signed by Gregorio Martínez Sierra in a prominent position in the living room. She recalled having read several of the novels as a teenager while living with María in France. She had said to her aunt: "You must have written this, auntie." According to Margarita, María would simply smile and reply: "Possibly child, possibly." She showed me envelopes containing letters to María from Manuel de Falla, Juan Ramón Jiménez, Ramón Pérez de Ayala, Joaquín Turina and many others. She also had numerous letters from Gregorio to María and another bundle of letters from María to her family.

As I read the letters from Gregorio, I was struck by his delicate but expert manipulation of María. It became quite clear too, that, ironically enough, she had written much of what Catalina's splendid acting had brought to life. These two women were, in effect, the real pillars of Gregorio's fame as well as his fortune. He orchestrated — if not exploited — the talents of both and was a genius at making them function at peak efficiency. Gregorio, little more than five feet tall and very slightly built, must have had enormous magnetism and energy to have captivated so completely these two extraordinary and different women and to have managed so successfully his considerable business enterprises at the same time. Friends who knew him suggest that his very fragility worked in his favor with both María and Catalina and call his power over them "the strength of the weak." Without wishing to detract from Gregorio as writer, director, or businessman, it seems that his major and most lucrative talent was discharged as entrepreneur of two major properties: María and Catalina.

In addition to establishing beyond any doubt María's active authorship, Gregorio's letters demonstrate a lively concern with business matters. While he was frequently solicitous of María's health, he constantly urged her, albeit apologetically, to send him new works, complimented her on material he received, and chided her gently if she was not actively writing. On tour, he urgently needed new plays and suggested that writing would make her feel better. Despite the separation from Gregorio occasioned by his amorous and professional alliance with Catalina Bárcena, correspondence proves conclusively that María continued to mail to various parts of the world plays which she wrote alone and which he performed and published, with her blessing, under his name alone. A selection of illustrative excerpts from letters of Gregorio Martínez Sierra to María follows, revealing both the workings of the collaboration and Gregorio's manipulative handling of the situation.

VIII   *From the Letters of Gregorio to María*

I think it's fine that you don't write if you aren't feeling well, or if you want to rest after having worked so much. Therefore, I didn't even remind you of the short amusing lectures which are what I would have needed most, or the monologues that we outlined in Paris, or the third act of "Carola tiene suerte" ["Carola Is Lucky," unpublished, available in the University of Cincinnati Library], which I would have liked to perform in Buenos Aires to give them the first fruits of a work, which would have been much appreciated. I repeat that it is perfectly fine with me that you haven't done anything if you are ill or tired, but that you abandon two plays because they seemed "too daring" [the two works in question were probably *The Devil's Hour* and "Spell", the latter an unpublished play about a homosexual performed in Buenos Aires in 1930] seems absurd to me. We have performed and continue to perform *Ivory Tower* everywhere with success. I planned *The Devil's Hour* badly; I asked you to fix it up in Paris, and you told me absolutely that you didn't want to touch it and that you preferred to write another new one. So I didn't insist. We can write and perform all the plays that are good, no matter how daring they may be, in my company, in Artigas's or anyone's. If you work only an hour a day without having to hurry or feeling any pressure, you can write two or three plays a year without even noticing. I advise you to write because, after all, that's our profession. The theater companies are more difficult every day, and in order to continue with mine, I need new plays because I've already told you we've performed everything. Since you couldn't or didn't want to write anything, I have worked with and continue working with Marquina and Honorio [Maura] in order to nourish our repertory.

. . .

Yesterday I reread the first two acts of "Carola tiene suerte," and I'm thrilled to death. They have a serenity, a sobriety, a quality so honest, and so modern, such deep emotion, . . . I would really like you to do the third act these days in Madrid, so we can perform it in Barcelona, which is undoubtedly where they have the most taste for this type of play. In Paris we will work on the lectures so they'll be clear in our minds and well planned, and then they'll be less work for you.

. . .

I forgot to tell you in my last letter that the collaboration has been arranged — four articles per month — in Mexico City, Mérida, Havana, Buenos Aires, and Chile. And there will be many others. I am absolutely certain that we will get five hundred pesetas for each article. I have told everyone that they will be letters to women and dialogues. And the collaboration will begin in May or June. Let me know by return mail if I can continue to make firm committments. The important thing is that all the newspapers publish the articles on the same date; to regulate the deliveries we will need to have twenty finished before sending them. They can be shorter than *Letters to the Women of Spain*: four or five typewritten pages, and sometimes less, according to the theme. Let me know if you will be able to have the first twenty ready at the end of April, or when.

. . .

I have just read the second act of *Ivory Tower*, and I think it's wonderful. Besides being very theatrical, it has a very excellent modern and personal literary quality, refreshing charm, emotion, depth, purpose, style, quality; nothing's missing. I think it will be one of our best plays. The female character, healthy, courageous, strong; the character of the man consists of not having any, since he is always a reflection of the girlfriend or the mother, and especially the mother, present in body and soul, as you were telling me, through the anguish of the son; everything well done. The tutor is very good — and it was a difficult scene — and the assistance of Rafael and Inés — the ending is excellent. And it's a very Spanish play, since that terrible mother is and especially was so often repeated — I'm really happy. Congratulations. The third act won't give you much trouble because it is perfectly defined in the novel. As soon as they are copied we'll begin rehearsing the first two acts.

. . .

Of course I am waiting impatiently for the third act of *Ivory Tower*, but I'm not worried because I am sure that it will be good. You're really working well: everything you've done lately has vitality, constant interest, and great charm, which is the most important thing.

. . .

I really liked your idea; it gives meaning to the play, and it's delightful. For the main plot, take advantage of anything that you find interesting, and especially not commonplace, of everything I told you. Until you tell me how you're going to put it together, I don't want to advise you on anything because with this plot I seem to go toward trivial things; on the other hand, what you do is very nice. It could be emotional and lends itself to poetry too. When you tell me the general outline, I'll intervene with suggestions or modify whatever occurs to me. Now it will have the double charm of traveling from Spain to Venice and back.

Some advice, that I also gave you when you wrote *The Peacock* [a play attributed to Marquina]: try not to have too many characters; have main characters and do without incidental characters (unless they are really outstanding): this makes the performance easier and saves a lot of money in costumes, which are very expensive.

Don't worry about making several scenes short and intense: I have had some ideas about quick changes, and the sets aren't expensive, now that I only have to pay Burman. In *The Peacock* people really liked the scene changes, and it's probably easier for Marquina to write a play with a faster pace.

. . .

The third act of *The Devil's Hour* is perhaps the best of all, and you know how much I liked the first two. It couldn't be better. It has emotion, strength, tension, interest, poetry, everything that's good. Even the storm and the rain at the end are effective. I think it's a great play, and I'm sure the public will like it very much. I want success, as always, but I'm so certain of the quality and value of this play that I'm not even worried.

. . .

I repeat that you're writing better than ever. Which means that when you've recuperated totally, in complete possession of your physical faculties, you will write masterpieces, if you don't become too bourgeois now that you are living on "unearned" income.

. . .

I didn't receive "Hay que ser feliz" [i.e., *Seamos felices (Let's Be Happy)*] until yesterday: it took a long time to get here. I liked it very much: it's superb. And surely it will be a big success. Without any vanity I can say that we're the only truly modern Spanish authors. Our characters live and think in an up-to-date way. This play couldn't have been written twenty years ago. Actually the same is true of our older plays: they seem contemporary. On the other hand, our colleagues continue completely in the nineteenth century.

. . .

Today I read "Hay que ser feliz" [i.e., *Seamos felices*] to the company: an enormous success. Everyone was enthusiastic. I really liked reading it aloud. It will be a tremendous success. Especially in Buenos Aires where the women are intelligent and aware. The third act — besides the success, which is unquestionable — will give them a lot to talk about. The men will say that the husband shouldn't return without certain conditions. The women, on the other hand, will love it. This play will be around for a while.

IX   *María's Motivations*

From the time of her wedding in 1900 until Gregorio's death in 1947, María chose to publish all of her considerable production under her husband's name. María may have elected, subconsciously, to conceal her identity behind the name of a man to avoid the resistance or hostility of the conservative Spanish audiences accustomed to male dramatists. Although theater people and friends were aware of the writing arrangement, María maintained a public reserve about her authorship that ranged from romantic to stubborn to perverse and — at times — to foolish. Why did she refuse credit? Was her ego dormant, underdeveloped, or simply repressed?

While the "male ego" has long been identified, the "female ego" has yet to assert itself in sufficient quantities to become recognized, let alone become a platitude. For centuries little girls the world over have been taught modesty, passivity, docility, and selflessness as appropriate, feminine, and hence desirable, qualities. Girls, as future mothers, have been taught to serve, to share, to give, to speak softly, to hide intelligence, to repress leadership tendencies, to stifle creativity, to avoid calling attention to themselves, and to control anger. The cardinal maternal (and feminine) virtue, according to this repressive system, is putting the needs of others, especially men, first. Corollary to the feminine "virtues" are the feminine "sins" of competition, assertion, aggression, pride, and worst of all, success in areas men have coveted as their own. In other words, the qualities and accomplishments the system has considered proper and admirable for men are abhorrent in women, and vice versa. Because of their social conditioning, women have been especially receptive to the Christian insistence on self-abnegation. The obedient and religious young María must have received many a lesson in the soul-saving properties of humiliation in the face of pride and the edifying effects of self-denial. In addition, she must have taken these lessons to heart.

Considering María's formation in a stoic and militantly Catholic land of women martyrs and legendary maternal sacrifice, her reactions seem almost predictable. Moreover, the self-effacing attitudes apparent in María the woman find an echo in the maternal nuns of the dramatic works. These heroines, shaped principally by María, no doubt, have one outstanding trait in common: renunciation of self. It is also quite possible that work became a substitute for María's ego as well as for the love she did not receive from Gregorio. If nothing else, she sublimated her anger and frustration in a strange yet productive way: through oddly calm and optimistic literary works.

If Gregorio did not love María in the conventional sense, he certainly needed the work she offered without conditions or threats. Unlike Catalina who said she would leave the theater company if Gregorio did not live with her, María did not suggest reprisal. In addition to abating somewhat María's loneliness, writing provided insurance against total abandonment by Gregorio. Work filled the void, became her crutch, and surely provided a sense of dignity and self-esteem that she otherwise might have lacked. Much like the renunciation motif of the plays involving nuns, the work ethic is woven into the fabric of almost all of the novels, stories, and theater. In the mildly feminist plays, work (ideally performed with the husband) is equated with happiness. Although equal partnership is a central issue in these works, María failed to apply the concept to her particular situation. She may have let heart — as well as upbringing — overrule reason when it came to proclaiming her true importance in the collaboration.

A major irony of the rejection of credit is María's feminism. Had María revealed herself formally as an author, she might have inspired other women to follow her lead. Moreover, writing was a profession she strongly championed for women. Her situation was, in fact, the reverse of that of the typical woman writer. If a Spanish woman attempted to write fifty years ago, one might expect the rumor to circulate that certainly a man was assisting if not actually writing the material (the case of Concha Espina, for example). María's insistence that all work was accomplished in collaboration with Gregorio may have been an expression of her own desire — a way of denying the painful reality of separation. After 1924, the "collaboration" was perhaps something of a myth, a fantasy she promoted and found comforting. While in a small sense Gregorio continued to work with her (he encouraged and offered suggestions), physically and emotionally he was thousands of miles away.

Why did not María clarify the collaboration she refers to only tangentially in *Gregorio and I?* Did she think that formally revealing her major contribution would be unladylike and somehow disloyal to her husband? Did she think that clarification would be tantamount to discrediting a dead man? Was she so totally lacking in artistic and personal ego that she wanted no credit? Did she enjoy being a martyr? Was she continuing to spite the family for the lukewarm reception of her first book? Or was she simply the loving and generous wife who wanted all credit to go to her husband? Was María's love for Gregorio largely maternal? Did she always see him as terribly young, weak, and insecure? If she wanted the secret of her major writing role to endure, why did she not destroy the telling letters? Was it because María, still sentimental, couldn't destroy this final and tangible evidence of Gregorio's affection and need for her? Or did she secretly hope that her authorship would one day be established?

Why did she accept — and apparently without a struggle — Gregorio's involvement with Catalina Bárcena? Why did she continue to write and mail him plays and essays — which he performed and published under his name with her blessing — years after he had left her to live with Catalina? Was María a shy woman whose principal interest was writing? Was her relationship with Gregorio purely literary? Did she prefer the anonymity that publishing under a man's name provided? In some perverse way, did María enjoy the speculation about her writing role? Would a public pronouncement have spoiled her little game and perhaps have made people wonder if she really wrote the works they seemed willing to concede to her without actual proof?

Although María Martínez Sierra's active authorship is now a certainty, many questions remain unanswered. With a smile which I envision as proud, stubborn, stoic, and perverse — yet kindly and maternal — Spain's foremost woman playwright has taken to the grave answers to these and other riddles related to the mysteries and complexities of human personality.

CHAPTER 3

The Apprenticeship Years: 1898–1910

IN the final decade of the nineteenth century, Spanish readers showed a preference for sentimentality and the evocation of mood through delicate rhetoric. Precisely because the early works of Martínez Sierra so thoroughly represented the tastes of the period, they are little read today. In these times of anguish and catastrophe, readers tend to demand an earthier realism expressed in violence, explicit sex, and four-letter words. Martínez Sierra's works, Modernist in style, idealistic, languid, pantheistic, moralistic, and melancholy in tone, run directly counter to current trends. As Ricardo Gullón notes: "All that was imprecise and could evoke nostalgic and melancholy moods was used by the Modernists, and of course, by Martínez Sierra, whose natural inclination to sentimentality was almost dangerously encouraged by the climate of the period."[1] Gullón goes on to suggest that the personality of Martínez Sierra may have failed to evolve completely and ventures the possibility that he continued in several ways always to be a child.[2]

Martínez Sierra shows a general kinship to early twentieth-century writers who praised nature as an antidote to encroaching industrialization. Unlike the writers of this group who saw factories and machines as the enemies and dehumanizers of man, Martínez Sierra wrote in a characteristically positive and optimistic way, accentuating the advantages of the simple life led in harmony with nature. Using a verbal palette lacking in harsh colors, he painted comforting pastel landscapes devoid of violence. Perhaps because he had lost faith in traditional religion, Martínez Sierra sought a universal order — and hence solace — in the beauties of nature. Recalling John Ruskin, he shows that this beauty has morally beneficial effects on society as well as the individual. Unlike Ruskin, however, he does not specifically condemn material progress as the natural enemy of human happiness.

"What Martínez Sierra does suggest, however, is that in cities or in large crowds, there is decreased opportunity for direct contact with nature; God's message is therefore muted. A humane mystic somewhat akin to Fray Luis de León, this writer flees from the "worldly noises" of the city to a natural refuge of beauty, order and balance. Work is recommended as a salutory and desirable form of human consolation, but unlike his plays, many of the novels and stories end on an unhappy note. While the praise of work continues throughout his works, the pessimism of the early period vanishes in the more optimistic dramas.

Because access to these all-but-forgotton early works of Martínez Sierra, limited almost exclusively to large university libraries, is so difficult, I will review them briefly in this chapter. Although not vitally important in the history of Spanish literature, these early works are basic to the total scheme of Martínez Sierra's literary production in that they document a gradual rejection of certain styles and attitudes and a consequent evolution toward others while basic outlines of character, structure, and ideology emerge. Of particular importance is the formulation of the maternal ideal of self-sacrifice and the shift in attitude of women characters from pessimism and defeat in their limitations to a position of optimism and strength. The Spanish woman presented in the early works — while not yet the feminist heroine of the plays — is admirable in several novels and stories for her noble and strong qualities. The weak, vacillating male, also a frequent character in the successful plays, takes form in this period as the rather consistent foil for the superior Spanish woman. This weak-willed man naturally gravitates toward the protective maternal qualities exemplified in Martínez Sierra's feminine ideal.[3] Toward the end of this early period, the villain-antagonist emerges in the conservative Spanish woman, a negative representation of what Martínez Sierra believed women should be. Frequently cast as the mother of adult children and the fierce preserver of convention and tradition, this character resembles Gregorio's mother as described by María in *Gregorio and I.*[4]

I   *The Modernist Dialogues*

Although Benavente assisted with the publication of *Labor's Poem*, his public sponsorship by way of the prologue was reserved — if not imperious and disdainful. Suggesting that the youthful Martínez Sierra had attempted more than he accomplished in this first effort, Benavente writes: "He sings of human strength, life and work; he is eloquent more for feeling than for words. Those of you who leave the temple disappointed, those of you who convert the religion of art into political science for life, do not smile in disdain at the fervent newcomer, and do not try to get him to pray in your congregation with ritual formulas. Allow his aspirations to be superior to his strength. All ideas should be inaccessible."[5] In commenting on these words of the prologue many years later, María, with her customary good humor, writes: "And that means in plain language: "This work isn't much.""[6] Nevertheless, both Gregorio and María were grateful for even this reserved and slightly arrogant support.

These allegorical prose poems, written largely in dialogue, extol the work of men and nature, and in style indicate that the author has drunk from Modernism's fountain. The first piece, entitled "The Immortal Legend," begins in this fashion: "Night was falling. There, on the line of the horizon, where shortly before the turquoise heaven melted in harmonious union with the azure sea, a wide swath of light, a dazzling atmosphere of innumerable golden particles stood out boldly as the sun swayed slowly and majestically before sinking into the curling waters that tremblingly reflected the sun's image and which, as it drank the final rays, crowned the broken wavy crests with an irridescent diadem of changing color glittering with silver sequins."[7]

In this majestic, natural setting, the poet places the beautiful figure of a woman — symbolic of the poetic muse — who laments her imminent demise at the hands of Logic and Science (i.e., modern technology). A chorus of workers then voices a hopeful song in praise of work: "Don't cry, don't fear that inspiration will fail because Legend, of splendid clothing and mystic expression, has died. Let her fade away quietly in the waves, wrapped in her shroud of beams, for what does it matter? In place of her soft and sad sagas, sing the beautiful poem that never dies, the heroic epic that never ceases, the beautiful and ever-new legend, the one that brought men together and forged nations, the one that does not sleep encased in haze; the one that creates, cheers, renews and ennobles: The Legend of Work."[8]

In a subsequent chapter entitled "The Immense Embrace," the allegorical union of Work with Idea takes place. Work struggles toward Idea, a beautiful form that resides on the crest of a very steep mountain. When Work finally scales the mountain to embrace Idea, Art is born of the union. In this fashion, Martínez Sierra, in a progressive and regenerationist mood, recommends work as an indispensable ingredient in the production of beauty in life.

In the final piece of *Labor's Poem*, an epilogue entitled "Disappointed," nature again provides the background for a parable concerning love and the gift of artistic creation. As two dreaming young lovers watch jellyfish floating on the surface of the ocean, the youth, anticipating his beloved's desire, leaps into the sea to claim the prize for her. The current is treacherous, however, and swirls around him. When he finally conquers the waters, captures this token of devotion, and places it at the feet of his loved one, he sees that he has given her but a formless mass of jelly. Although the gift is not what he had envisioned, the girl takes it in her arms and smiles as she exhalts the value of intent (i.e., work) over result: "You struggled to get it for me and that is enough."[9]

Gregorio's contribution to *Labor's Poem* may represent the jellyfish that the young poet places at the feet of his flesh-and-blood (as well as very active) muse, María Lejárraga. The idea was luminous and beautiful; he dreamed of making her a splendid gift worthy of his love, but reality fell short of the idea (as Benavente suggested in his prologue): "I wanted to put it [the gift] at your feet wrapped in rainbows, perfumed by the aromas of fortune, surrounded by a halo of sunbeam rays and dew drops, girded with foam, lulled by waves of hope, caressed by love's breezes . . . a gift worthy of you." Disappointed in his accomplishment, he completes the epilogue with: "It [my work] is worthless but represents my efforts to please you; it is work undertaken with so much love and so much enthusiasm, engendered in my spirit always swept along by the mysterious, irresistible attraction of your deep gaze."[10]

In its political and cultural overtones, *Labor's Poem* can be compared to the attempt of the Generation of '98 to confront the problems of an ailing nation. Unlike other works of similar inspiration produced by members of the Generation of '98, the ideological thrust of *Labor's Poem* is positive, enthusiastic, and determined, which is unusual for this period of crisis and tremendous questioning. Indeed, *Labor's Poem* overflows with the enthusiasm, optimism, and reverence for work that were to characterize Gregorio Martínez Sierra, the dramatist. In its poetic language, symbolism, imagery, and delicate tone, this work represents Modernism in form as it reflects the concerns (but not the attitudes) of the Generation of '98.

Nine years later, however, in a 1907 speech in the Ateneo of Madrid, Martínez Sierra made this observation about *Labor's Poem:* "Don't read it if you have the chance: it has 122 pages — sincere, of course, but with a rash of adjectives that would stand your hair on end. . . . *Labor's Poem* had some success with the Socialists; a certain critic even called me a thinker — he really believed it. I was praised in *Blanco y Negro* [*Black and White,* a popular Spanish magazine], and Anarchist friends flooded the house. They of course fled when they realized what an individualist I was."[11]

In addition to helping Gregorio publish *Labor's Poem,* Benavente admitted him to his circle of friends and invited him to join his Art Theater Group. In subsequent years, Benavente and Martínez Sierra would perform in plays together and become warm personal friends. Early in the relationship, Benavente gave further evidence of his confidence in the Martínez Sierra writing talents. Manuel Salvi was then publishing a series of literary *instantáneas* ("snapshots") and invited illustrious writers to contribute pieces based on a theme suggested by a picture. When Benavente saw that a train had fallen his lot, he passed the picture along to the Martínez Sierras with the suggestion that they write something appropriate. Rather than take offense, Gregorio and María accepted the challenge gratefully. When they saw their carefully elaborated prose published above the signature of Benavente, their joy was boundless.[12]

The *Diálogos Fantásticos (Fantastic Dialogues,* 1898), written in prose, are nine lyric, symbolic exchanges dedicated to Benavente, the first literary benefactor. Reminiscent of the traditional *autos sacramentales* (allegorical plays that exemplified the Church dogma, principally the Eucharist), the "speakers" (i.e., "characters") are Life, Death, Heart, Head, Soul, Truth, Fairies, Muses, Work, Idea, etc. Of the *Dialogues,* María writes: "In them, without realizing it, we were imitating our immortal Calderón who, three centuries ago, brought to life with human feeling and passion, abstract figures and mere theological concepts."[13] A characteristic dialogue of this collection entitled "Work of Love" returns to a theme of *Labor's Poem,* for here Work again pursues Idea who resides on a remote and inaccessible mountain. Although Idea coyly tries to elude her suitor, the latter persists and finally overcomes her. Work weds Idea, and the creatures of the plain joyfully announce the inevitable product of their union: Art.

Martínez Sierra's third work, *Flores de escarcha (Frost Flowers*, 1900), dedicated to the Modernist poet Salvador Rueda, who had contributed the prologue to the *Fantastic Dialogues,* contains twenty-four short stories in free verse that continue in the symbolic, languid, moralistic vein of *Labor's Poem* and the *Fantastic Dialogues.* Nature continues to play an important role, but there is a more decadent, pessimistic quality to this work that separates it from the mainstream of Martínez Sierra's writings. While Goldsborough Serrat calls *Frost Flowers* superior to the first two works, I must agree with María who, late in her life, judged this work rather harshly: "Those flowers aren't worth anything."[14] The critic Leopoldo Alas (Clarín) ridiculed *Frost Flowers* at the time of its publication, but when he served on a panel of judges for *Almas ausentes (Absent Souls)*, he praised the latter saying: "I never would have thought that Martínez Sierra could write a novel like that."[15]

In an early "flower" (story), Nature, ever the refuge of the sensitive, invites the poet's spirit to join her in an abode high above the earth. Nature verbalizes here a characteristic Martínez Sierra dichotomy-synthesis of realism and idealism as she recommends: "Let your body be a prisoner of Earth — but come up quietly, gently, piously; come up and look at the Earth from the heights and you will see that it is beautiful seen from above. Give me your hand, come up with me, poet, my beloved singer of songs, and hear my lesson."[16] Later, in "Rhapsody," a four-page dialogue of the Soul with Heavenly Voices, Memories, and Desires, Martínez Sierra attempts to parallel the rhythm of Liszt's Second Rhapsody.[17] This experiment in simulating musical patterns through poetry was frequent practice with the Modernists.

Another of the pieces, "Spoliarium," calls to mind a sonnet that Juan Ramón Jiménez was to write some time later: "Octubre" ("October"), from his *Second Poetic Anthology.* In the Jiménez work, the poet sees the farmer drop seeds into the furrow and thinks of the golden wheat which will flower in time to attest to the quality of the seed. He is then tempted to tear out his own heart and drop it in the furrow, believing that the tree of eternal love which would spring forth would give living and palpable proof of the quality of his feelings. In Martínez Sierra's "Spoliarium," the poet, full of love, yearns to make some sacrifice as proof of his devotion. He decides to write beautiful poems about the stars, summer nights, clouds, and storms; but humanity repays his devotion by calling him a fool. He then turns to songs of the earth to praise clay, forests, and streams; but humanity this time mocks him for glorifying commonplaces. Desperate because no one understands his love, he decides: "With my own blood shall I sprinkle the fields where I want the blessed grain to spring forth." Believing that if people do not see love in the abstract, they may recognize it flowering before them concretely, the poet sings, here, his most intimate and heartfelt song, playing, as it were, his finest card. The golden grain flowers, but still no one understands. In their rage, the people shout: "A soul! A soul! The soul of a poet sung in verse! What pride! Let's destroy the prophet who prefers his soul to the heavens and the earth. He is the devil!"[18] They kick the poet, insult him, and crush the skull that harbored the heresy. As mentioned before, *Frost Flowers*, in its cynicism as well as pessimism, is uncharacteristic of Martínez Sierra.

II   *Early Prose Fiction*

Absent Souls (1900) is Martínez Sierra's first attempt at the novel. The narrator, a writer desiring to learn more about the mentally ill, spends some time in an insane asylum. He comes to know the director, Pedro, and his assistant, Lorenzo, a saintly man who devotes his life to the care of the sick. The latter loves Anita, who in turn loves the artist, Ortueta. Although Lorenzo feels his love for Anita is hopeless, he unselfishly protects her (without her knowledge) in meetings with Ortueta. On the night of one of their trysts, an inmate kills Ortueta. Lorenzo feels that somehow Providence has directed the murderer, for he senses that on this night Ortueta would have tried to seduce Anita. Lorenzo, witness to such a scene, would not have hesitated to protect Anita even if it meant killing Ortueta. Lorenzo now leaves the asylum because he feels that Anita may turn to him, and since he has made a vow to sacrifice his own life to care for the insane, he will not permit himself the luxury of Anita's dependence and devotion.

This work, reminiscent of a gothic novel with its ghostly, castle-like asylum, its glimpses of tortured souls, and the floating image of the sweet, innocent, oblivious heroine, Anita, abounds in metaphor and poetic prose. The action moves fairly swiftly, however, through Romantic description and Realistic dialogue. This selection will suffice to give an idea of the tone of the descriptive passages: "The moon, conqueror of the clouds, shone again. The asylum emerged slowly from the shadows; first its Moorish towers loomed bright, then its embattled flat roofs; then the light ran rapidly and spread out, like a mantle of snow, to illuminate the building, top to bottom."[19]

Absent Souls shows a trend toward a simple rather than complex plot, with a preference for describing moods and personalities rather than actions. Because simplicity and mood are difficult to sustain or extend, Martínez Sierra has been more successful in the short, contained forms, like the sketch, the short story, the novelette and the drama, rather than the novel. In *Absent Souls* he also shows a preference for reality, rejecting the allegorical approach of the first works. Both content and language shift from the poetic and the symbolic toward the mundane, a direction that was to continue.

Pursuing the short novel, Martínez Sierra produced *Horas de sol* (*Sunny Hours*) and later included it in his Renacimiento collection of short works, artistically printed in small volumes (intended to be given as gifts rather than, for example, flowers or candy). The same collection included short works by such established writers as Clarín, Galdós, and Valera.[20]

Sunny Hours (1901) is the romantic story of a wealthy, aristocratic city girl sent to the country for a vacation. There, in the sensuous yet pure atmosphere of raw nature, Hortensia falls in love with Carlos, a simple village boy. As in other works of this period, there is a pantheistic note, and the sun works its special magic. Hortensia seems mesmerized, almost inebriated with the warmth and life-giving force of the sun. The omniscient author, fusing the heroine with the other beauties of nature, describes her under the summer sun as: "lost, one knows not how, in the orgy of light, converted by magic arts, perhaps, into just another atom of all those infinite atoms hypnotized and put to sleep by the power of the sun."[21] Hortensia takes long walks with Carlos, who thinks as he looks at her: "How the savoring of nature invites to love, and how the warm soul opens our eyes to the beauty of the Earth!"[22] The author, in an aside to the reader, comments: "And he was happy imagining that the glorious pantheism of Hortensia was the work of his love."[23]

Under the spell of the sun and the beauty of nature, Hortensia believes that Carlos is the man destined to share her life. When she returns to the cottage one afternoon, however, a letter from a friend in the city thwarts nature's course. Amelia writes of the many festive parties in Madrid and that all her friends miss her. She also makes fun of the friends who have laughingly suggested that Hortensia might be having a "country idyll." Hortensia, a victim of *el qué dirán* ("what people will say") thereupon rejects her natural inclinations and decides to return to the city immediately. The novel ends, thus, on a sad rather than a happy note.

In the Ateneo speech of 1907, Martínez Sierra made this interesting observation: "*Sunny Hours* is something of an eclogue written under a luminous, inebriating summer sun; . . . the end of the story is somewhat like the end of a nap: pessimistic. Love vanishes like a dream and the protagonist is left feeling angry at herself for having dreamed; if I wrote that story again now, perhaps I would allow love to triumph. Juan Valera, in the marvelous vitality of his last years, was of the opinion that it should have triumphed. If you read this work, I'll leave it up to you whether or not to read the last page."[24]

The novel *Pascua florida* (*Easter Sunday*, 1903) suggests a subtle variation on the theme of the return of the prodigal in its opening pages. In her early youth, Josefina had foolishly married a gambling, unreliable foreigner who had made her life miserable. Now a young widow, she returns to her mountain village to draw solace from her roots. Martínez Sierra illustrates some xenophobia in sketching the characterization of Josefina's husband. Because of his strong belief in the Spanish virtues, only a foreigner could be portrayed as so demoralized.

In the village, Josefina lives with Don Antonio, her kindly schoolmaster grandfather and is exposed to the healthy influence of a neighbor, Lucita, the real heroine of the novel. Lucita (whose name "Little Light" suggests her role as the beacon) lives with her bachelor brother, Lorenzo, a doctor. When Josefina returns to the village, she cries and wants to be alone. Lorenzo treats her coolly at first but urges her to be more like his sister, who immerses herself in various good works in the town and lovingly cares for Don Antonio. The implication is that work is Lucita's solace, for when busy and needed, she has no time to be sad. As spring approaches and the sun summons nature from its lethargy, the schoolmaster recovers, and on Easter Sunday, Josefina and the doctor realize that the pleasant relationship that has developed between them is love. The novel ends on the optimistic and happy note of rebirth, new beginnings, and love.

Despite her very traditional role in caring for her brother and the old schoolmaster, Lucita anticipates in her strength the positive attitudes and assertiveness of the modern Spanish woman illustrated in the Martínez Sierra theater (specifically Julia of the first play, *Life and Sweetness*). Although not a nun, she demonstrates qualities common to the religious heroines: renunciation of self and a need to care for something or someone. The doctor of *Easter Sunday* (apparently reflecting the author's attitude) thinks that his sister, constantly the consoler, has been created to caress and to mitigate pain.[25] She has grown especially fond of the old schoolmaster and explains: "It is because I have taken care of poor old Don Antonio that I have taken such a liking to him . . . he was like a small child you have to rock."[26] In this statement she anticipates Sister Juana of *Cradle Song*, who loves the Lord as one loves a small child. Sister Juana dreams of trying to hush the cries of the baby Jesus with lullabies. As Martínez Sierra constantly suggests, women love and nurture by instinct; indeed, they often fail to separate romantic love from this urgent need to take care of someone or something.

Lucita seems to have little prospect for marriage, a fact that depresses her greatly. She fears being ridiculous and alone in her old age with only a lap dog to caress. Woman's lot — surprisingly, when we consider the optimistic heroines of the later works — is not portrayed as a happy or even a hopeful one. No resistance to the situation becomes apparent, however, until the feminist essays[27] (beginning in 1916) and the theatrical illustration of the modern woman's rights and responsibilities. Making the point that work only distracts Lucita from her own frustrations and that she indeed needs the problems of others to occupy her mind, the omniscient author intervenes: "The fact is that as Lucita's friends conquered their problems, she would sink slowly and silently into the waters of depression."[28] Commenting on the misfortunes of Josefina, Lucita echoes a sentiment reiterated subsequently in *Still Water* (1909) as she says: "They should strangle female babies at birth."[29]

The symbolic use of nature, especially the sun, is frequent in these early works. Martínez Sierra seems to say that the warmth of the sun is a basic human need, psychologically as well as physically.[30] When spring comes and the sun warms the earth, hope and love blossom, and everything takes on a rosy, optimistic hue. With the coming of spring, therefore, the old schoolmaster conquers death, and the young couple reaffirms faith in life and love with their plans for the future. While the sun plays a rather subtle role in this work, it plays a major and dramatic one in *Dream Theater* (1905).

Sol de la tarde (*Afternoon Sun*, 1904), with a prologue by Santiago Rusiñol, collects into one volume several short works previously published in various journals: "Golondrina de sol" ("Sunny Swallow"), "La monja maestra" ("The Teaching Nun"), *Horas de sol* (*Sunny Hours*), "Aldea" ("Village") and "Los niños ciegos" ("The Blind Children"). In 1907, Andrés González Blanco called *Afternoon Sun* the pinnacle of Martínez Sierra's career. He praised his delicately phrased feeling for nature and his ability to paint landscape with words.[31]

"Sunny Swallow" can be considered a forerunner for both *Cradle Song* and *The Shepherds* because of strong similarities in ideology and plot. An old priest and his sister adopt a young gypsy boy whose only preoccupations are with the physical aspects of life. The priest and his sister, on the other hand, prefer to concern themselves with the child's spiritual needs. The priest realizes, however, that one cannot minister to the soul or seriously consider the hereafter until basic needs — food and shelter, at least — are satisfied. In "Sunny Swallow" it is the kindly old priest rather than his sister who, in his charity and unselfishness, personifies the maternal instinct so important throughout the works of Martínez Sierra. While the sister is not one of the tyrannical and unattractive women devoid of kindness often represented in Martínez Sierra's theater,[32] she remains suspicious of the gypsy lad and warns her brother that he will some day break his heart. The priest and the child represent the dialectics of body and soul; the now versus the hereafter; the hunger for life versus the hunger for eternity. The boy, much like Teresa of *Cradle Song*, is true to his blood. When a gypsy caravan passes through and invites him to join it, he hears the siren song of his nature (much as Teresa hears the call of earthly love in *Cradle Song*) and gives vent to his natural tendency to live on the open road, a vagabond. When the priest discovers the absence of the child, he, like Sister Juana in *Cradle Song*, feels a great void and cries in the final scene of the story.

"Margarita en la rueca" ("Marguerite at the Distaff") compares two sisters, one paralitic and incredibly selfish (Engracia) and the other loving and sacrificing (Margarita). Margarita is engaged to marry Pedro but delays the wedding because her invalid sister continues to need her. Faced with a choice between Pedro and Engracia, Margarita elects to suppress her own desires in the interests of her sister. She is, then, a classic, self-sacrificing, renouncing heroine. Pedro eventually marries someone else because his farm needs a woman's hand. After many years, Engracia dies and Margarita seeks out a heavenly spouse. When she goes to the convent to present herself, she is told that no one over forty is admitted. As she turns sadly away and walks under a sunny sky apparently indifferent to her suffering, all she can think is: "Don't you want me either, Lord?"[33]

In "The Teaching Nun," another story of feminine renunciation, the title character renounces worldly pleasures for a life of dedication to young girls. She is a precursor of Sister Gracia of *The Kingdom of God* in the joy she takes in mothering her young charges. Unlike Sister Gracia, however, she is anguished because she lacks a traditional belief in God. Although her confessors recommend much prayer and work to overcome this failing, Sister María Jesús, like other nuns in Martínez Sierra's theater, needs human love to make life meaningful. She consoles herself that delivering souls to the Lord may compensate for her own shortcomings. One day, one of her charges confesses with much difficulty that she is "bad"; she no longer wishes to hear Mass or receive communion because she cannot believe. Fearing that she has projected her own lack of faith — and hence eternal damnation — on an innocent soul, Sister María Jesús faints. The story ends abruptly with the anguished cry of the young student.

In "Aldea" ("Village"), Juancho, an *indiano* (a Spaniard who comes back from America, usually wealthy) returns from Cuba to his native Asturias. Amidst lyrical descriptions of misty green hills that plunge into the sea, Martínez Sierra suggests rather than develops a love triangle. Juancho falls in love at forty with his beautiful, exuberant young niece Malia. She, however, rejects his tentative advances, even though her friends suggest she marry him for his money. Juancho's dream of love evaporates suddenly as he overhears Malia's laughter and rather spontaneous acceptance of the advances of a young village boy. As the story ends, Juancho is left pondering the merits of having sacrificed his youth to financial — but solitary — security. Andrés González Blanco calls "Village" the best story in this collection and finds that it exemplifies not only Martínez Sierra's excellent prose style but his ideological and literary doctrines as well.[34]

The final story of the collection, "The Blind Children", takes place in an institution for blind children, operated by nuns. José Luis, fourteen, lost his sight at the age of eleven, while Toñín, thirteen, has never seen. A significant detail of the story deals with Toñín's attempt to understand light and to visualize the sun, almost an obsession in these early works. When asked how he imagines the sun, Toñín says that it must be something like the "smell of flowers that enters through the eyes."[35] Sister Gracia, a young nun who watches over the boys, is a special favorite of both. As in "The Teaching Nun," Sister Gracia anticipates the characterization of Sister Gracia of *The Kingdom of God*. Here, however, we see her through the eyes of the children. One evening, the young nun calms Toñín in his troubled sleep. When she puts her hands on Toñín's brow, he takes her hand, kisses it and licks her fingers. José Luis, disturbed and jealous of Sister Gracia's attentions to Toñín, takes his friend to the woods and suddenly pushes him down an embankment into the river. Although he calls for help immediately, Toñín is dead before anyone can reach him. That night, José Luis has a nightmare, and Sister Gracia comes to calm him. In a burst of guilt, anger, desire, and anguish, José Luis crushes Sister Gracia's hands in his and bites them until the blood bathes his face. The story ends as Sister Gracia flees, screaming in terror. The abrupt ending with the frustration of the central character also recalls "The Teaching Nun." Although I have dwelled largely on recurring themes and ideas in *Afternoon Sun*, Martínez Sierra's love for nature and his penchant for painting the landscape in a poetic and idealized fashion — characteristic of the early period — are much in evidence.

III   Dream Theater

Teatro de ensueño (*Dream Theater*, 1905) is the first published attempt of Gregorio and María at theater. Because the pieces in this collection are experimental and Modernist, they were not performed at the time. These poetic sketches were, however, given a sumptuous resting place in a beautiful volume with a cover painted by Santiago Rusiñol, a prologue by Rubén Darío and the inclusion of lyrical verses by Juan Ramón Jiménez. Also included in the first edition of *Dream Theater* was *Saltimbanquis* (*The Tumblers*), a work that subsequently was set to music by Usanizaga. The musical version of *The Tumblers*, like *Las golondrinas* (*The Swallows*), *El amor brujo* (*Love's Sorcery*) and *El sombrero de tres picos* (*The Three-Cornered Hat*), has become a standard item of Spanish musical theater and continues to be performed regularly in various parts of the world. The other three brief theatrical pieces of *Dream Theater* are: "Por el sendero florido" ("Along the Flowery Path"), dedicated to Benito Pérez Galdós; "Pastoral," dedicated to Benavente; and "Cuento de labios en flor" ("Story of Lips in Flower"), dedicated to the Quintero brothers. Each piece is accompanied by poems by Juan Ramón Jiménez that were later included in his *Pastorales* (*Pastoral Poems*, 1911), published, incidentally, by Martínez Sierra's publishing firm, Renacimiento.

The first short piece of *Dream Theater*, "Along the Flowery Path," deals with some of life's harsher realities on an idealized and lyrical plane. While Dinko is traveling through Spain with his little Hungarian circus, Mirka, his wife, dies of starvation and overwork. In this sketch, Martínez Sierra again asserts his often-reiterated belief that one of woman's duties is to console; she must smile even when sad, and her laughter must give comfort and joy. As Dinko says of his wife: "She was our joy, always laughing."[36] Because Mirka represented life and happiness to Dinko, he rejects the idea of her death and, unable to bear this final separation, refuses to allow her burial. Dinko's father finally convinces him to proceed with life because Mirka would not have wanted him sad. He consoles Dinko by suggesting that Mirka is now part of nature: "Those who have left us and love us do not want us to cry. . . . Look at the light that is coming up behind the mountain. It is she, it is Mirka, who is coming to console you."[37] Again illustrating the pantheism so much a part of his early style, Martínez Sierra suggests that Mirka has not ceased to exist; she simply exists in another form. She has become a part of all nature. Mirka now will be associated with light, with beginnings, and with the smiling encouragement and warm energy radiating out from the sun. This happy resolution became typical of Martínez Sierra's optimistic philosophy of life.

"Pastoral," a Modernist allegory of humanity's search for wisdom, is divided into four "seasons" (acts) representing man's chronological age and progress toward maturity. In this poetic piece dedicated to Benavente, young Alcino — "Everyman" — lives in a wintry kingdom of ice and snow. Having heard his elders speak in reverent tones of a warm kingdom ruled by a beautiful and fair Sun Queen (symbolic of the exotic, distant, and mysterious things that human nature, in its folly, seeks), Alcino abandons the security of his cabin to go in search of her. On his journey, he is joined by Rosa María, a young girl from his village who loves the shepherd unselfishly. As they travel toward warmer climes, they pass through the Time of Spring. Rosa María explains her devotion for Alcino to the queen of this region: "I stay close to rid his path of thorns and to pluck flowers for his forehead."[38] Alcino, untouched by Rosa María's devotion, thinks only of the Sun Queen. The Spring Queen recognizes Rosa María's authentic love and warns Alcino of his folly: "Zephyrus, crown her [Rosa María] with roses because she knows how to love. And you, shepherd, don't you know that it is insanity to disdain the love that comes to you in preference for some vague future happiness?"[39]

When Alcino finally reaches the kingdom of the summer where he supposes his Sun Queen reigns, he learns from the workers that theirs is a monarch without a country. She travels to all lands (i.e., the sun shines on all countries indiscriminately, belonging exclusively to none). These workers exemplify the recurring idea (suggested already in *Labor's Poem*) that they are favored rather than disadvantaged people. While the Sun Queen travels to all lands and belongs to none, she favors especially the workers because it is they who till the fields and encourage the fertility of the soil. Precisely because the Sun Queen loves abundance, she love those who tend her fields. One reaper, specifically relating work to consolation, invites: "Take the hoe. Work is a good companion of hope."[40] He suggests, as did *Labor's Poem*, that work and accomplishment go hand in hand to produce art and happiness.

Alcino, however, not having been born wise, must suffer to learn. He is soon tempted by the promises of the grapes; they assure him that life, warmth, and joy are to be found in wine. Seduced, Alcino abandons Rosa María to give in to debauchery. In the final scene, Alcino, once again in his family's cabin, hears Rosa María relate how she found him abandoned and nearly lifeless at the side of the road. As Alcino looks at Rosa María now, he realizes for the first time that she is the rosy-skinned, blue-eyed, golden-haired Sun Queen that he had sought all along. Rosa María then takes leave of him, for as Opportunity she had knocked but found no response. She may pass his way again, but never in the same form. His task is to recognize her various guises. This work, much like Maeterlinck's *Bluebird* or Baum's *Wizard of Oz*, tells us that happiness is always at hand; we simply fail to see it and foolishly seek it in distant lands. He suggests that we are blind if we chase exotic dreams, for happiness is more a function of the person than of other people and is always within our grasp. Our task is simply to recognize it.

The characters of "Pastoral" are forerunners of those repeated frequently in later years. Alcino, at the same time that he symbolizes mankind, is a weak and undiscriminating Spaniard who can be lured into drunkenness because he fails to recognize happiness in the form of a good Spanish wife. In this narrower sense, Alcino is the allegorical Spaniard looking abroad for the woman of his dreams. After hard and painful travels, he returns to recognize Rosa María, the girl with whom he could now, in his maturity and wisdom, be happy. Similar characters, situations, and conclusions are found in *The Hopeful Pilgrim, Adventure,* and *You Are Peace.* Queen Anisuya of *The Mute Jungle* also makes the mistake of falling in love with a foreign prince, and in *Easter Sunday,* Josefina found only misery in her marriage to a foreigner.

"Cuento de labios en flor" ("Story of Lips in Flower") is the least "theatrical" of the pieces, the most poetic, and most appropriate for a medium not yet invented: the technicolor motion picture. With almost as much descriptive material as dialogue, this short play illustrates how two sisters, Blanca and Rosalina, fall in love with a painter. Their love for each other, however, is superior to the love they feel for the young man. Each believes herself to be preferred by the painter and therefore a cause of pain for the other sister. As they bathe in a stream fed by waterfalls, the sisters illustrate Martínez Sierra's ideal of feminine renunciation as they simultaneously submerge themselves to die for the happiness of the other. The river carries the bodies, which seem suddenly to become two water lilies. In some mysterious way the girls are reunited in nature.

"The Tumblers," dedicated to Santiago Rusiñol, begins with a poetic illustration of Juan Ramón Jiménez (as do the other selections) and presents traveling jugglers and actors who perform in village squares. The principal characters are Lina, youthful, optimistic, always smiling and laughing; Cecilia, a sultry, ambitious beauty; Puck, the man both women love and who must choose between them; and the poet Juan Ramón Jiménez, who plays himself among these fictitious characters. In the first act, Puck and Cecilia are in love, but the latter, a brooding representation of pride reminiscent of Benavente's Imperia (in *The Witches' Sabbath*) decides to leave the troupe to make a name for herself. She considers the small circus a world unworthy of her talent. In the second act, four years have passed since the departure of Cecilia, and Lina, who had playfully tried to reconcile Puck and Cecilia whenever there were problems, realizes that she is in love with Puck. In his own way, Puck loves Lina, but he continues to dream of and be dominated by the memory of the beautiful Cecilia. Juan Ramón Jiménez, in a dialogue with the now melancholy Lina, assures her that sadness is superior to happiness, for the latter is surely a vulgar sentiment. He reasons that the tragic moments of life remain with us while the happy ones seem to fade from memory. Since what is truly worthwhile is enduring, he asserts, sadness must perforce be superior to happiness.

As Act 2 ends, we learn that Cecilia, now a famous star, is the feature attraction at a theater in which Puck and the troupe will soon perform. When Cecilia sees Puck again, she declares her love for him and succeeds in luring him away from the company. Puck, abhorring himself for his own weakness, foreshadows the ending as he tells Cecilia that he is disgusted with himself and wishes he could kill Cecilia or die. Lina is dejected, feeling that she has lost Puck. Very soon, however, a wild-eyed Puck comes to confess that he has killed Cecilia. Although disdainful at first, when Lina learns of Puck's desperate predicament, she maternally forgives all and swears to share whatever fate is in store for him.

Although this play was at first rejected as not sufficiently commercial, it certainly was in harmony with the predominantly melodramatic works of the theater of the early twentieth century and, as María Martínez Sierra points out, could have very well been written by Echegaray, Guimera, Rusiñol or Cano.[41]

IV The Humble Truth *and* You Are Peace

La humilde verdad (*The Humble Truth*, 1905), with a title inspired by a novel of de Maupassant, is one of Martínez Sierra's few attempts at the long novel. This work was written especially for a contest in which it won third prize.

Paco, a wealthy, restless village youth, decides to go to Madrid to study. His *cacique* (town political boss) father indulges his son in this whim, believing firmly that the boy will find the village much superior to the city. Paco's sweetheart, Elena, the town beauty, displays much apprehension at Paco's departure, for she fears losing him to a pretty and sophisticated city girl. In Madrid, Paco does find a new interest in the daughter of the boarding-house mistress, but she is hardly the person Elena — or perhaps even Paco — had envisioned. Very soon, however, the less romantic city girl announces her bethrothal to one of the older boarders. Disappointed, Paco returns to the village but without enthusiasm. The father fails to understand why Paco cannot be happy as the son of the town's most important person.

On the final page of the novel, Martínez Sierra hints at the reasons for Paco's vague discontent. Giving a new and realistic ambiance to the theme of his first work, *Labor's Poem,* the author suggests that we truly appreciate only what we have acquired with our own effort. When Paco's father insists that he is the village "prince" and heir apparent, the narrator interjects: "And the son thinks that it is a sad kingdom that has not been won with one's own effort, and that this kind of royalty will never, never satisfy him."[42] Because of the attention elicited by *The Humble Truth* as third-place winner in a novel contest, the Barcelona publishers, Montaner and Simón, invited Gregorio to write a novel for a special collection they were preparing for families. Although Gregorio and María were about to leave for France, Gregorio accepted the contract. While in a Parisian boarding house, they wrote the requested novel, *Tú eres la paz (You Are Peace,* 1906), their most popular work except for *Cradle Song.* This novel would reach a wide reading public of sighing young girls in both Spain and South America during the first part of the present century.

If Gregorio was not involved with Catalina Bárcena in 1906, this novel was a coincidence and also proved to be uncannily prophetic (except for the novel's happy ending). The triangle pattern that had been vaguely suggested in previous works ("Village," *The Humble Truth,*" "Pastoral," "Story of Lips in Flower," "The Tumblers") became more defined, and the characters — even their names (Ana María and Carmelina) — suggested the real-life triangle that would eventually emerge between Gregorio, María, and Catalina. In *You Are Peace,* the central figure, Ana María, modest, intelligent, optimistic, gay, and self-controlled (her name as well as her character suggest María), is in love with her artist cousin, Agustín who, while abroad, has fallen in love with a beautiful model. Carmelina (whose name and profession suggest Catalina) is much like Cecilia of "The

Tumbers" as well as Imperia of Benavente's *Witches' Sabbath*. (Here, however, she is a minor character and we learn most about her indirectly, much as we learned about Josefina's foreign husband of *Easter Sunday*.)

Ana María and Agustín, partially reared by their grandmother, had declared their love for each other prior to Agustín's departure. As the novel opens, Ana María and the grandmother (this kindly figure of many successful plays establishes her prototype here) await the return of Agustín. Because in his absence Agustín has stopped writing, Ana María faithfully composes long, newsy, affectionate letters and passes them off as Agustín's to keep the grandmother happy. When Agustín returns, Ana María and Agustín, in order to preserve their grandmother's happiness, pretend that their relationship has not changed and that they will eventually marry as planned.

An interesting novelistic technique utilized in this work is the telling of the story from various points of view. The third-person narrator describes the pleasant rural setting and much of the action. Direct contact with reactions of the characters is provided through letters that Ana María and Agustín write to friends. The reader thus sees not only an objective description of what has taken place but subsequently views the scene as other characters have perceived it.

The novel revolves principally around the interaction between Ana María — proud, unselfish, maternal — and Agustín, the rather weak-willed young man who ultimately recognizes his need for her. Ana María's superior Spanish qualities are further enhanced by direct comparison with those of a foreign woman; Carmelina visits the village briefly to give to Agustín the son they have had and to beg him to return to her. Now that Agustín has had a chance to compare the two women, he realizes that he loves Ana María. (She also, of course, reacts tenderly to the child.) Because of the child, however, he feels a responsibility to return to Carmelina. But before Agustín can leave, he receives a letter from Carmelina saying that she has decided to travel with a foreigner she has just met. At this point, Agustín, freed of obligation to Carmelina, declares his love for Ana María. Amidst real wedding plans, the grandmother dies never knowing that there had been a separation between her grandchildren. The pious lie told for love and the relationship of role-playing to reality are situations and ideas that Casona utilized in *Los arboles mueren de pie (Trees Die Standing)*. The great similarities in the situation suggest that perhaps Casona knew and admired this work of Martínez Sierra.

You Are Peace has a much more modern air than previous works. In addition to being quite realistic in setting, there is less description; the dialogue is the normal language of young people, and there are fewer rhetorical sentences couched in poetic, symbolic prose. Here, too, flesh-and-blood characters rather than symbols emerge strongly. Ana María is the prototype of the woman the Martínez Sierras admired and would portray again and again in the theater. In addition to being Spanish (a very important virtue), this character is intelligent, modest, quietly aggressive, long-suffering, self-controlled, smiling, and gay. Juxtaposed to her is the prototype of the undesirable woman: not only foreign, she is designing, frivolous, unmaternal, and amoral. Agustín is a pleasant young man, but extremely weak. He needs a mother, and Ana María is quite willing to oblige.

V Gregorio's Poetry and the Final Novels (1907–1910)

Gregorio's single volume of verse, *La casa de la primavera* (*Springtime House*, 1907) — bearing the simple dedication: "To María" — is divided into four sections: "Ballads of the Home" (eleven poems), "The Romantic Cities" (five poems), "Spiritual Landscape" (twenty-four poems), "The Message of the Roses" (two poems) and "The Hours" (four poems). Forming a preface to the book are poems by several established poets: Rubén Darío (who dedicated one of his most famous poems, "Song of Autumn in Spring" to Gregorio), Juan Ramón Jiménez, Antonio Machado and Francisco Villaespesa. A 1912 edition of *Springtime House* adds another poem by Enrique Díez-Canedo.

The title of many poems as well as of the entire work were suggested by Juan Ramón Jiménez, who also frequently suggested names for Martínez Sierra novels, stories and literary heroines. The poems, uncomplicated lyrical praise of life's simple moments, hardly betray Martínez Sierra's early Modernist orientation. A few titles from "Ballads of the Home" suffice to give an idea of his unadorned, unsensuous, realistic songs of conjugal bliss: "My Beloved Makes Lace," "Our Chat One Sweet Morning," "The Laughter of My Dearly Beloved."

María Martínez Sierra remembered with special affection this work in which she was (she claims) exclusively muse rather than active collaborator. Reminiscing about the period in which her husband rhymed stanzas about white tablecloths, her small hands, and the simple joys of love, María fairly exults: "My husband was writing verses about me! And I'm not exactly a dream; I'm more reality; I'm not a distant goal but a constant presence; not an impossibility but daily bread."[43]

Beata primavera (Blessed Spring, 1907) is a novelette that illustrates ironically the life-giving properties of warmth, sun, spring and physical attraction. As the prospective murderer of a king awakens, he notices that the rays of the sun irritate him as they filter through the window. He feels that on such a historic day, the weather should recognize his act and be severe and overcast. He prepares the dagger and leaves to have coffee before carrying out his plan. It is carnival time, and the king is to make an appearance. As he leaves the café, he brushes against a woman and automatically begs her pardon. In the manner of her reply, he recognizes the prostitute. The revolutionary feels some disgust at this proof of corruption and thinks that his dagger may bring a better world for many. Again in the crowds, the "hero" is jostled and once more encounters the prostitute. This time, she aggressively asks him why he is thinking so seriously. Inspired, he walks with her as he expounds on progress, happiness, knowledge, justice. She listens in silence, but when they are far from the crowds, she kisses him. Suddenly realizing that it is too late to kill the king, our hero resigns himself to the next best thing: a night of love. Somehow the sun, the warmth, the crowds, the temptation of life have conquered thoughts of death. The narrator's final comment seems quite out of character for either Gregorio or María: "Thus a king was saved through the graces of a prostitute, which goes to prove that it is in the interest of the reigning dynasties to preserve in the royal domain these poor sellers of their bodies, who, on given days, are successful in making people laugh at opportune moments."[44] The story does not focus on the man's intent to murder as an expression of libido or on the ironies inherent in seeking life through sexual contact at a time death had been planned. It focuses, rather, on the coincidence of the situation in a rather light-hearted manner.

In *El agua dormida (Still Water,* 1907) a small girl views life around her. An ironic vision of adulthood, the life of the mother is seen through the innocent eyes of the child. Resembling Lucita, of *Easter Sunday*, without the crutch of submerging her own misery in the problems of others, the mother seems weak and unable to cope with her life. In reference to women in general, she frequently says, "How unfortunate we are." At one point, she attempts to take her own life and that of the little girl (whom she may be attempting to save from the pain of womanhood) by jumping into a canal. The novel ends with the little girl's remembering that her mother said to her, as she was putting her to bed: "When a woman is born, someone should knock her head against a wall."[45]

Aventura (Adventure, 1907) is a short novel set against the background of an Asturian festival. Pedro, a thirty-year-old bachelor, returns to his native region after living in Madrid to find his parents urging him to marry a local girl. Imagining their selection would be a chubby rustic, Pedro looks for excuses to return to Madrid. Quite by accident, he encounters the beautiful, slender, and coquettish Marcela splashing almost nude in a pond. When he approaches and attempts to kiss her, he finds that she aggressively defends her honor. She is, in short, the Martínez Sierra ideal; attractive, outgoing, modest, and not only Spanish, but from the hero's home town as well. Because Marcela is the young woman Pedro's parents had in mind, the novel ends on a happy note amidst preparations for a wedding.

In *Ivory Tower* (1908), a novel later dramatized (1924) under the same title, Martínez Sierra combines characters that persist in his fiction: the working-woman mother (frequently personified in two separate characters in other works); the tyrannical, conservative mother, antithesis of the ideal; and the weak-willed man who gravitates to feminine strength and seeks in his wife the comfort he never had as a child. The aristocratic Gabriel leaves his ancestral home in the north of Spain to study for his doctorate in Madrid. There he falls in love with a seamstress, Mariana — warm, feminine, and maternal — who gives him the support and affection he needs. Mariana treats Gabriel somewhat like a helpless, beloved child and encourages him to attend class and work hard. Although she and Gabriel live together, she does not allow him to support her and insists that she must work. Gabriel comments: "Don't tell me again. I know already. I'm familiar with your 'nobody supports me but me.' Pride, pride."[46]

After having their child, Mariana, weak and ill, is unable to play her managing role. Gabriel, overcome with the responsibilities thrust upon him, regresses to an infantile state psychologically. The narrator interjects: "And the recently born manly spirit of Gabriel, as though the prey of furious dogs, succumbed, falling again into the limbo of childhood; a fearsome childhood as his had been, tormented by formless and nameless ghosts. Oh, that unavoidable fear! Fear of might, of light, of death which doubtless was hidden in the bedroom, fear especially of what he most loved, of Mariana, predestined, perhaps to die. Fear of himself, dragged by her and with her."[47] Like the "absent souls" of the novel by the same name, Gabriel's weak psyche is broken and he retreats into a neutral world, a limbo without joy, pain, rights, or responsibilities. It is at this moment of despair that the dragon-mother learns of her son's situation and whereabouts. Believing that Mariana has stolen the body and soul of her only child, she dramatically swoops down to exorcize the evil spirits.

At the time of the mother's arrival in Madrid, Mariana is ill with a high fever. The delicate Gabriel, depressed about Mariana's condition and shocked by his mother's visit, simply faints. The mother then has Gabriel's preceptor, who has accompanied her on the trip to lend moral and physical strength, carry the unconscious Gabriel to the carriage.[48]

Once home in Santander, Gabriel's will is completely broken. He rises late, eats little, and spends the day lying in a hammock. He makes no attempt to return to Madrid or to contact Mariana. On the other hand, Mariana, pale and weak, comes to Gabriel as soon as she is able. In her maternal way and unconcerned about her own abandonment, she has worried about him and asks only: "Can he be sick?"[49] When she finally speaks to Gabriel, he sighs and looks at her forlornly. Further revealing her maternal orientation, Mariana lifts Gabriel's face and murmurs: "Let's see that face. Look at those eyes. Of course I know what's the matter with you. It's pure jealousy of the little one, thinking that now all the spoiling will be for him and just him. But if you are very good, maybe there will be some for you. Isn't that right, baby, that we are going to love your father a little?"[50]

Even the marchioness is astounded that such a devil can seem so innocent and thinks to herself: ". . . this woman laughs like a child, her eyes shine and she says to her child and mine the same affectionate, simple, singing, childish words that good mothers say to their children born in the bosom of God's law."[51] But then she decides that the devil's evil trick is to come disguised as an angel of light. At this point, both women confront each other to dispute, as it were, possession of Gabriel, each woman wanting to "save" him. Gabriel's escape is again loss of consciousness. For the marchioness, salvation is another life after death. For Mariana, salvation is in life; she hopes to save Gabriel from "death, insanity, and sadness." Attempting, perhaps, to make the mother a character rather than a caricature (reminiscent here of Martínez Sierra's mother as seen through María's eyes, incidentally), the narrator explains some of the mother's pathology. Married quite young to an insensitive man who immediately went his own way to spend money on women and vices, the embittered and lonely young woman had turned to Gabriel, displacing her hostility (disguised as protection) on an already sickly child.

The confrontation of the two women and the expression of their divergent points of view sets Martínez Sierra's vitalism, humanism, and optimism in sharp focus. The marchioness has sublimated all desires and frustrations into religion and even wears a habit. She is indeed the negative archetype of the traditional wife whose background separates her too much from her worldly husband to be his partner either sentimentally or intellectually. Convinced that she is doing battle for an immortal soul, the marchioness refuses to relinquish Gabriel. Mariana, conceding defeat, takes her child and returns to Madrid. That night, when the marchioness is occupied with penance and prayers, Gabriel dresses and, just as he had as a child (the infantile syndrome continues), jumps from the window to the garden. He takes a horse from the stable and sets out for Madrid. The horse stumbles, and Gabriel is killed. When his lifeless body is returned to the manor house, however, a smile lights his face, for in death, life has somehow triumphed. Gabriel's final act, at least, has been a manly one.[52]

Like the marchioness and Gabriel, Mariana is a character that will recur in Martínez Sierra's works. Although not quite the feminist heroine (she does not attempt to invade the professional areas dominated by men), she earns money honorably through her dressmaking business, takes pride in her independence, and is a happy and positive person. Gabriel suffers from that common ill so often documented in the novel of the Generation of '98 and frequently associated with *abulia*. He envies Mariana her abundant strength of will and determination. Mariana chides him and reminds him that he is a man in addition to being wealthy and titled. A forerunner, perhaps, for the feminist heroine, Mariana displays frustration at limitations placed on her as a woman:

If only I were a man. But it's better not to think about it, because I'd never be able to stop telling you. First of all, I'd travel the world over — I don't know — go as far as China. Imagine, with the world as big as they say it is and only having seen just a little bit of it — but where can anyone go with skirts? Would you believe, sometimes I'm tempted to cut my hair, dress like a man, and just travel around, even if only as a puppeteer? And if one wants to work a little bit, a man, even if he's born in the orphanage, can be an important government official, while a woman, you know, about the best thing she can do is teach kids, or be an actress and starve to death when she gets old or be a prostitute and die of repugnance in the hospital.[53]

This speech sounds very much like a confession by María, the feminist, the lover of work, the inveterate traveler and lover of puppets.

El peregrino ilusionado (The Hopeful Pilgrim, 1908) is a short novel written in a mixture of dialogue and a narration. Reminiscent of Maeterlinck's *Bluebird,* it tells of a young Spaniard who travels to many distant lands in search of the ideal woman, feeling that ascetic, arid Castile could not produce the woman of his dreams: "If wise, she is not feminine; if ignorant, she can't be pleasing; if pious, she forgets to smile; if sinful, she forgets to sigh."[54] After speaking to women all over the world, he returns to Spain and meets a woman who wisely tells him with a smile: "The best thing about voyages is the return home," to which he replies, "You are the only woman who has ever understood me." She explains: "Because I am a Spanish woman and you are Spanish. See how sad the countryside is and how solemn the sky is? Don't you think that this monotonous land and changeless light make love promise to be — and feel — eternal?"[55]

The poetic dialogues of *La selva muda (The Mute Jungle,* 1909) suggest that the work was written about 1900 and not published until much later. It features the same languid style and romantic allegory of *Labor's Poem,* with the pessimistic note of *Frost Flowers.* Anisuya, the jungle queen, initially feels content in her natural environment. Accentuating the pantheistic focus of the work, the voices of the forest tell her: "Your heart is our heart, and in each of

our bows lies a fiber of your flesh."[56] Into this Garden of Eden —
symbolic, perhaps, of Spain — come men from northern Europe
who invite Anisuya to visit their country to learn of their more
"civilized" ways. Like Eve before her, Anisuya yields to temptation
and abandons her jungle in quest of knowledge. Although during
her stay abroad, Anisuya eventually learns that civilization thwarts
man's natural goodness, she falls in love with a prince. When he
proves false she returns, thoroughly disillusioned, to her jungle
home. She calls out to her old friends, but the jungle is silent; in her
search for something better, she has lost the innocence that gave her
happiness and allowed her to communicate with the creatures of the
forest.

In *Todo es uno y lo mismo (All Is One and the Same,* 1910),
Teófilo, a young college teacher romantically in love with his
superior's young wife, goes to Granada to rest and try to forget his
frustrations while the professor is on a research trip abroad. In a
Granada boarding house, he recalls his love for Teresita, the dark-
haired and very Spanish wife of his professor as he observes the
pale, tall, large-footed, awkward English women who are fellow
boarders. He finds the English girls especially unappealing because
they are so different from his typically Mediterranean love,
Teresita. In this section, Martínez Sierra caricatures the English
through humorous, ironic, and slightly hostile descriptions.

Subsequently, however, he meets Maud, and although antagonis-
tic to her at first, he keeps her company on several occasions. One
day after lunch, they both drink coffee which spoils their customary
siesta. Teófilo goes out to the balcony he shares with Maud and is
joined there by her. Soon they retire to her room and make love. In
similar situations (termed by Teófilo "mercenary" — but here he
does not pay, of course), Teófilo has kept Teresita beyond the
threshold of his mind so as not to offend her sacred image. On this
occasion, he imagines that Maud's hair is black rather than blond
and asks her to close her green eyes so that they will not remind him
that they are not Teresita's brown ones. "All is one and the same,"
he seems to conclude cynically. "All the pleasures of the world are
voluptuosity and nothing more than voluptuosity."[57] He feels
somewhat guilty about having ravished Maud (imagining her to be
Teresa) but rationalizes the act in his defense of a woman's right to
end her virginity whenever she chooses: "I believe that all the
virgins in the world are in their perfect right to stop being virgins

when they choose and in the company of the person that pleases them without the necessity of laws or blessings and without society's having the right to intervene with censorship or, heaven forbid, penalties. . . . It would be a fine thing if laws or opinions impeded the individual, man or woman, from sweetening life with whatever honey seemed sweetest."[58]

Teófilo is rather confused in this novel, but quite typical of men in the works of Martínez Sierra: slightly vacillating, he is definitely attracted to women whom he consciously or subconsciously sees as mother figures. Teófilo lives with his mentor, the professor and father figure, and suffers an Oedipal jealousy as Teresita retires at night with her husband. He suffers, too, when he sees her emerge from the conjugal chamber sleepily in the morning. He tries to make himself believe that she sleeps alone in spite of the double bed that occupies the room. Teófilo prefers to cast Teresita as a sibling and imagines her, like him, a disciple and adoptive child of the professor — or, at most, a platonic companion.[59]

Toward the end of the novel, Teófilo receives a maternal letter from Teresita in Australia that instructs him in the care of her bird, her plants, and the house. She includes her husband in an affectionate farewell and, as a mother might, shows concern for his health: "Don't work too hard and get sick."[60] Teófilo immediately abandons Maud to rush to do Teresita's bidding, and as he remembers her concern for his health on the train to Madrid, he muses: "I too would like to be a child and go to sleep in your arms, my darling; because the embrace that takes form in the air should be for you. I want to be yours."[61] Despite his romanticism, the novel ends on an ironic and slightly humorous note as Teófilo confesses: "I did have a good time on that little convalescence trip!"[62]

El amor catedrático (*Love Is The Teacher*, 1910), the concluding work of the apprenticeship period, expands upon *All Is One and The Same*. Here the Martínez Sierras return to the technique of telling the story from various points of view which they had employed in *You Are Peace*. The triangle relationship is again utilized, but this time two men love one woman. While letters were interspersed in *You Are Peace*, this novel utilizes predominantly an omniscient narrator. The form of *Love Is The Teacher* is generally epistolary and subjective in tone. Although it also uses much dialogue, there is, unlike *You Are Peace*, little description of nature.

In the first section, Teresa — a young woman who bears a remarkable similarity to the youthful María Martínez Sierra, physically and ideologically — writes to a friend about falling in love and marrying her college archeology professor. In the second section, Teófilo, the godson and academic protégé of the professor (with whom he has lived since childhood) recounts how he had fallen in love with Teresa when they were college classmates. When she marries the professor and comes to live under the same roof, Teófilo's anguish becomes acute. In the third section, the forty-five-year-old professor muses about love and being married to a student twenty-five years his junior. The fourth and final section, the account of Teófilo's encounter with an English girl in Granada as he attempts to forget Teresa, had already been published independently as *All Is One and the Same*. Although both works were published in 1910, certain factors indicate that the novelette was composed first and then expanded (backward rather than forward in this case) to form the longer novel. The exposition contained in *All Is One and the Same* would have been quite unnecessary had the longer novel been written first.

All four sections explore attitudes of the characters, particularly as they relate to the role of women, and were very likely a prelude to the feminist essays. In its rather disciplined stream-of-consciousness, reflective way, this narrative is as akin to the essay as to the novel. Despite the seriousness that one generally associates with the essay, there is a light-hearted tone here characteristic of the theater of Martínez Sierra's maturity. More than any other work of this early period (with *You Are Peace* running second to it), this novel bears, in my opinion, most traces of María's hand. In addition to reflecting her optimistic, gay, playful spirit, similarities between Teresa and María suggest that the character was a literary sublimation and a fantasy alter ego. In this respect, an interesting study could be made of the stylistic and autobiographical clues provided in a comparison of *Love Is the Teacher* with *Gregorio and I, A Woman Along Spanish Roads*, and María's correspondence with Juan Ramón Jiménez published by Gullón.

The inclusion of *All Is One and the Same* in *Love Is the Teacher* exemplifies the common practice of the Martínez Sierras and other writers of the day (e.g., Baroja, Valle-Inclán) of combining or extending sections of works into others under new titles. Several plays, of course, were based on earlier works: *You Are Peace* became *Madrigal; Ivory Tower* is both novel and play; *The Swallows* became *The Shepherds;* Sister Gracia of *The Teaching Nun* and *The Blind Children* also appears in *The Kingdom of God;* a part of the professor's section of *Love Is the Teacher* was published in *The Restless Life*. Without wishing to detract from the accomplishments of the Martínez Sierras, I must make clear that in addition to there being two collaborators, there is also substantial duplication in many of the works.

In the twelve years from 1898 to 1910, the Martínez Sierras evolve from poetic, languid, colorist, Modernist diction to a simple, direct, realistic approach. Throughout the period, however, they continue to encourage man to follow his natural instincts and to take pride in accomplishment. Indeed, the admiration shown for work in *Labor's Poem* will persist throughout all their writings. There is also a shift from lengthy descriptions of life and nature through allegorical dialogue to a concern for real people in more and more localized surroundings.

Reflecting a desire for the fusion of body and spirit embraced by a kindly cosmos to form a balanced and happy universe, Martínez Sierra casts nature, work, love, art, ideas, and people as a harmonious whole. Frequently symbolized in the sun, this balance is a positive beacon, a magnet that points toward a positive natural order. All things seem to demonstrate an innate harmony. One must only listen to the natural signals they emit. Man, then, will gravitate toward what is good if he simply allows nature to lead him. The noises, artificial light, and cement of the city tend, on the other hand, to obscure nature's message.

Because he showed a desire to submerge his soul in nature, some critics (especially Cejador and García Lorenzo) have compared Martínez Sierra to Wordsworth, Coleridge, and Shelley, the Lake poets of the nineteenth century. The affinity for painting the landscape with words and the interest in theater led quite naturally to the early association with the Catalan landscape painter and popular dramatist, Santiago Rusiñol. In his attention to detail and enjoyment of small things, Martínez Sierra can also be compared to Azorín.[63]

Just as the Martínez Sierras recall Rousseau in their insistence on the goodness of the natural man and the ultimate treachery of civilization and material progress, they also suggest D'Annunzio in their quasi-pagan joy of life and strong nationalism. They lack, however, the Italian's more refined enjoyment of sensual pleasures, for they were strongly moralistic and almost totally obedient to the bourgeois ethic. Their melancholy young men recall Goethe's Werther, and in the delicate imagery and Romantic expression of the inner life through poetic exchange, they show the influence of Maeterlinck. In the early period Martínez Sierra was, in fact, a curious amalgam of the poet, the pagan, and the mystic.

CHAPTER 4

Two Authors in Search of
Characters and Style

THE Martínez Sierras had approximated dramatic form in their early Modernist dialogues, *Labor's Poem* (1898), *Fantastic Dialogues* (1899), and *Frost Flowers* (1900). In the short plays of *Dream Theater* (1905), still Modernist in tone, they moved a step closer to theater, for these works, unlike the previous ones, were written with performance in mind.[1] Although no impresario was willing to risk the staging of such experimental works (see Chapter 1 for critiques), the Martínez Sierras optimistically continued to explore dramatic forms in exotic short dialogues and brief harlequin plays (*Illusive Village*, 1907; *Love's Enchantment*, 1908). Benito Pérez Galdós expressed an interest in presenting *The Ideal One* (1907), their one-act play concerning the pretender to an imaginary throne. Because the central character of this antimilitarist farce spoke much like Alfonso XIII, however, the project was abandoned.[2]

All of these quasi-theatrical experiments represented a flexing of artistic muscle; a searching for form as well as content. Although totally different from the sentimental, domestic comedy for which Martínez Sierra is remembered, these early works are interesting for the steady progression they document from symbolic, allegorical figures to flesh-and-blood characters, and from high-flown rhetoric to colloquial speech. Not theatrical in the commercial sense, the plays cast in dialogue are essentially poetic essays, while *Dream Theater*, Maeterlinckian, impressionistic, highly visual in thrust — and more appropriate for the contemporary art film — would have been difficult if not impossible to perform effectively on stage.

About 1907, the Martínez Sierras rather abruptly turned from the composition of colorist, Modernist pieces to focus on plays designed to please audiences. An important influence in this new direction may have been association with successful dramatists of the period, particularly Santiago Rusiñol, the Catalan dramatist and painter.

It was while the Martínez Sierras were in Paris in 1905 that they met Rusiñol, who wrote exclusively in Catalan, and accepted his invitation to translate *Buena gente (Good People)* into Spanish. Rusiñol must have been pleased with the results of the Spanish version of his play as well as with the personal association, for he subsequently invited his young friends to join him in composing an original play. Gregorio and María were especially happy about this opportunity, for Rusiñol's name guaranteed performance.

Because Rusiñol showed little interest in women characters, his role in building Julia, the central character of their work *Life and Sweetness,* was probably minimal.[3] On the other hand, Julia is precisely the prototype of the optimistic, attractive, and assertive woman that appears so frequently in the works of Martínez Sierra.

I Life and Sweetness

Life and Sweetness takes place in the home of Don Tomás, a university professor whose wife, Gertrudis, shares his enthusiasm for scientific investigation. Although their daughter Marcela attends the intellectual gatherings of her parents, she has other interests normal for a twenty-year-old girl. Marcela's parents hope that she will marry Dr. Dalmau, a member of their group, but Marcela finds him dull and prefers Enrique, a handsome and fun-loving friend not associated with her parents' group. The pace of the action increases when Julia, Marcela's aunt, arrives to spend a few days of rest in the country. Julia, like her brother, is a scholar, but she views research as a tool to enrich life. Because she disapproves of the sterile erudition of Don Tomás's circle, she quietly initiates a domestic revolution. By the final curtain, Julia has — as will many a future Martínez Sierra heroine — succeeded in accomplishing several changes. Dr. Dalmau also realizes that he and Marcela are not well suited, and one supposes that the latter will marry Enrique, the young man of her choice. Like the Quintero play, *El genio alegre (The Happy Genius,* 1906) and Benavente's *Los buhos (The Owls,* 1907), *Life and Sweetness* exalts vital satisfactions over purely intellectual ones.

II Youth, That Divine Treasure

In 1908, the first performed play credited entirely to Martínez Sierra, *Juventud, divino tesoro (Youth, That Divine Treasure),* enjoyed moderate success. Ideologically the mirror image of a much later and more popular play, *Rosina es frágil* (*Rosina Is Fragile,* 1918), *Youth, That Divine Treasure* centers, as did *Life and Sweetness,* around attractions and conflicts within a family. Emilio, an aging Don Juan, feels that he has at last found true love in Clara, his eighteen-year-old niece. Naive and inexperienced, Clara allows herself to be persuaded that she loves Emilio, but suddenly Pedro, Clara's cousin, appears for a visit. He is much attracted to Clara and succeeds in convincing her that youth should wed youth. The rest of the family then attempts to help Emilio forget his loss, anticipating the renunciation motif of the plays involving nuns in recommending that he devote his energies to helping others.

III Father's Shadow

Thanks to the support of the Quintero brothers, *La sombra del padre* (*Father's Shadow*) was staged in the Lara Theater in 1909. Set in northern Spain, as were many of the early nontheatrical works, this play features the return of a Spanish emigrant after seventeen years of hard work in Argentina (a situation explored in "Village" of *Afternoon Sun*).

Thoroughly materialistic and uncultured, Don José has a heart of gold and a strong belief in the validity of work, a frequent corollary of materialism. While in America, Don José had regularly sent money to his wife, Feliciana. He has, in fact, provided a luxurious life for her and their several children, now grown. Upon his return, Don José brings not only his rough, old-fashioned ways and a bag of Argentinian expressions (which may have amused audiences at the time), but Ernesto, a wild-eyed and primitive black servant, reminiscent of the stereotyped, shuffling Negro of early American movies.

Don José is strongly traditionalistic and paternalistic in his concept of the sex roles: he believes that the husband must provide materially for the family while the wife should contribute a spiritual and a moral orientation. He further believes that both parents should make whatever sacrifices are necessary to comply with their duties on behalf of the children. (In subsequent plays, the concept of sacrifice — particularly maternal sacrifice — would become a recurring theme.) Finding that in his absence the children have grown lazy and spoiled, Don José chides Feliciana for what he sees as her failure as a mother. She meekly replies that she has done the best she could as a woman alone. Don José rails: "Your daughters should not spend so much time without their mother knowing what they are doing."[4] He reprimands her for not having devoted sufficient energy to instructing the children and for not making more sacrifices. When she complains of fatigue and many sleepless nights, Don José replies: "Well, drink coffee and open your eyes. A mother should suffer for her children" (91–92).

The minimal action of this play centers on a dance to which the family has been invited. The children dress in their fashionable and elegant clothes while the father dons an old and ill-fitting tuxedo. When they indicate their displeasure with the father's appearance and suggest that he not accompany them, Don José decides that the whole family will remain at home. When the children pout, the father expresses disappointment. He fails to see that the children have simply absorbed the family's materialistic orientation without, quite naturally, having adopted the father's values regarding work. In addition to abandoning his family spiritually to provide materially (a decision that established his priorities), after his return he is constantly concerned that his son have plenty of money and even attempts to buy off the attentions of a female opportunist who is making life miserable for his married daughter. Since the father has provided so handsomely for the children and required no accountability, the children have led — and continue to lead — irresponsible and frivolous lives. They feel natural disdain for work and a certain embarrassment at their father's lack of polish, even though they know that his labors have provided their comfortable life.

Don José is portrayed as the patriarch while Feliciana is shown as the weak, indecisive, submissive — even whining — housebound wife. In the absence of the father, the family has naturally reflected the character of its only leader, Feliciana. During the seventeen years of his absence, the entire family has needed the involvement and authority of the father. Because the traditional disciplinarian has not been present, the family has lacked an essential order, a void impossible to fill even with maternal devotion. Indeed, Martínez Sierra stresses the importance of both parents in the formation of the children. Each parent, he suggests, has an essential function. Maternal softness, understanding, and protection, for example, must be balanced by paternal strength and decision.

When Don José finally realizes that he must assert his authority to save the family, the Martínez Sierras demonstrate an uncustomary lack of faith in the power of maternal love.[5] In addition, they imply that only a man can solve the problems faced by this family. When Don José asserts his authority, he hints at equality of parental responsibility in questions involving the children. Closer examination reveals that he gives his wife the right to command only when her words echo his own sentiments: "The father left the house, that's right, but he has returned, and from now on, nothing will be done in this house except what I say and what the mother orders, which is one and the same thing" (124). After delegating authority to Feliciana, Don José decides to ensure the salvation of at least one member of his family — significantly, a son: he will take Pepín to America where work has dignity and where he can become a "man" rather than a "playboy." Feliciana begs her husband to remain, saying that the entire family sorely needs the father's protective shadow. She tearfully adds that the children no longer need her and that if he abandons her now she will surely die. Although an atypically defective Martínez Sierra heroine, Feliciana does demonstrate more insight than her husband. At that moment, the sound of bagpipes drifts through the window. Don José nostalgically recalls the romantic days of his courtship and accedes to Feliciana's plea. His abrupt decision to remain in Spain somehow suggests that the recollection of his wife in a romantic context has effected his change of heart.[6]

While Feliciana is a rather shadowy and unsympathetic character, she does realize that the rearing of children is the joint responsibility of both parents. In this way she is admirable and superior to her husband, who in his bumbling insensitivity, is a typical Martínez Sierra male character. Father's Shadow, incidentally, is one of the few plays by the authors featuring a man as central character.[7] Precisely because this play demonstrates characters and attitudes unusual for the Martínez Sierras, it is a curious museum piece. Only as such is it interesting.

IV   Mistress of the House

In El ama de la casa (Mistress of the House, 1910), a play that in several ways is the reversal of Father's Shadow, the Martínez Sierras have found their style, their characters, and their message.

While in *Father's Shadow* the children had lacked the guidance of a father, in the subsequent play the children need a mother. The former play opposes a strong man to a weak woman, while in the present play, a strong woman (and a much more attractive and admirable character than Don José) is contrasted to a well-intentioned but essentially weak man. Moreover, the central character shines by comparison to several negative examples of the Martínez Sierra feminine ideal. In both plays, conflicts revolve around domestic problems that ultimately find solutions. Action in both is minimal, though it increases in *Mistress of the House*.

Carlota, a thirty-four-year-old childless widow marries Félix, a forty-six-year-old widower and father of three nearly adult (sixteen to twenty years of age) children. Félix's two daughters and a son have been without the guidance and affection of a mother for many years but have, on the other hand, been subjected to the antiquated, passively destructive influence of their maiden aunt, Genoveva, a sister of Félix's first wife.

The conflict of the play concerns the efforts of Carlota to establish herself as mistress of the house and mother of the children. Although the daughters offer resistance to their stepmother, the person who most resents her is Genoveva, for her position is being usurped. Very much a negative archetype of the conservative Spanish woman, Genoveva voices disapproval of Carlota as: "One of those 'now' women . . . the kind that works for a living . . . as an accounting clerk behind a desk. As if a decent woman had to earn a living! The woman should stay at home; but men . . . you know what I mean!"[8]

Carlota's father had died when she was young, and as her mother had received the traditional feminine education that prepared her only for marriage, she found herself in difficult circumstances as a widow. She had placed Carlota in an orphanage with nuns while she earned a living doing embroidery. As the play deals with Carlota's background, it anticipates aspects of *Cradle Song* and provides a retrospective vision of the orphanage from the child's point of view. Carlota had appreciated the nuns' caring for her but had longed for her mother and for a home. (Martínez Sierra may be suggesting that while the nuns of *Cradle Song* found Teresa satisfactory as a surrogate child, Teresa — whose feelings are not explored in regard to her mother — may have longed for the warmth of a home.) Shortly after convincing her mother to establish a boarding house so that they could be together, the mother died. Carlota then went to work, married soon, and, like her mother before her, was left a widow very shortly. After five years of working at another job, she had met and married Félix.

Carlota understands Félix's daughters' resentment of her attempts to make changes and to occupy their mother's place. She realizes, too, that her problems have been compounded by Genoveva's lack of involvement and discipline in the home. At sixteen and eighteen, both Gloria and Laura do exactly as they please, wear ridiculous false curls, wash infrequently, and use excessive makeup. Carlota finds the house dusty, unkempt, and disorderly, with the furniture badly placed and pictures hanging crooked on the walls. Félix and his son Ricardo are always in need of clothes and the laundry is not done regularly. Because meals are not served with an eye to appetite, digestibility, or punctuality, Ricardo frequently eats in a corner bar.

With so many projects to undertake, Carlota sets about with missionary zeal to put the house in order. She demands that the girls comb their hair simply and wash it more often. In addition, she assures them that they do not need to modify God's creation with unnatural cosmetic colors and false curls. To use such things, she says, is a form of lying (79). She sees that all have clean clothes, regular meals, and proper rest. While the women resent Carlota's involvement, the men appreciate it greatly. Ricardo, indeed, mistakes his filial gratitude for love, and in addition, Félix may have sought a mother for himself as well as for his children. Carlota happily tells him how to dress, lays out his clothes, sews on his buttons, and reminds him when he needs a haircut. She prescribes a stroll after dinner and long nights of sleep for his dizzy spells and brings a steaming cup of coffee as he awakens. In general, she attempts to bring physical order to the house and moral leadership to the family.

Initially Carlota's reorganization is unsettling: Aunt Genoveva huffily decides to leave; Carlota discovers in checking accounts that Félix's business manager is performing his duties inadequately; Laura wants to run away with her boyfriend; Ricardo declares he is in love with his stepmother. In the midst of these many crises, Carlota asks Félix if he trusts her absolutely to solve the problems that have arisen. He does, and Carlota — in her determination, activity, and optimism — becomes a composite Martínez Sierra heroine, combining maternal sentiments and authority with the active optimism of the heroines. Carlota's first act is to take over the business accounts of her husband. When Patricio, the accountant arrives, she informs him that she will oversee all paying of bills, explaining diplomatically that she wants to divide responsibilities with him. In a curious comment for these early plays when María was not yet active as a Socialist, Carlota clarifies with: "I am very much a Socialist" (60). When he complains that what she contemplates is improper for a woman, she answers good-naturedly but gives not an inch.

In a humorous crisis scene with Genoveva, the two women exchange insults. Genoveva, upset that she has lost authority in the house, accuses Carlota of materialism and of lack of respect for the memory of Félix's deceased wife. By such an accusation she refers to the polishing of the furniture, the cleaning of the house, and the provision of a comfortable and healthy home for the family. She suggests that Carlota's attention to the physical over the spiritual aspects of life is somehow sacrilegious and calls her "ordinary." Carlota makes a response that ideologically joins *Mistress of the House* to the next work, *Cradle Song*. Perhaps echoing María Martínez Sierra's own sentiments as a childless wife, Carlota defends herself as she voices the central theme of the play: "Ordinary or refined, a woman needs first to be a woman. And do you know what being a woman means? Well, it means being a mother, no more, no less" (71).

When her stepson declares his love for her, Carlota recognizes his well-intentioned mistake: "You don't love me so much. I mean, yes, you do love me, but not the way you think. I am the only woman in the world who has ever worried about you, the only one who has made life a little comfortable for you. You haven't fallen in love with me, thank God. You have fallen in love with ironed collars and clean clothes and pants without baggy knees" (86). Rather than suggest that there is more to love and marriage, Carlota tells him that there are other women in the world who sew on buttons as well as she and that some are even prettier and younger. She assures him that such a maiden is eagerly waiting to take care of him and make him happy. Although the ideas on marriage of the Martínez Sierras evolved, they consistently suggested that the good wife was largely maternal in the relationship with her husband.

Carlota solves Ricardo's problem by putting distance between them, suggesting that he study engineering in Belgium. Ricardo, much like the "poor John" character of future works (one bearing this title), loves women who mother him and accepts filially whatever she decides. Indeed, after accepting Carlota's plans for his future, Ricardo runs out to buy half a kilo of fresh coffee for her. He stammers: "Yes, ma'am, just as you say, anything you want . . ." (88). Carlota then turns her attention to other problems and solves them with similar ease and efficiency.

When Félix sees that his wife has solved all of the domestic crises as well as some of his business problems, he says simply: "You are right; you are an admirable woman" (81). As the play ends, Félix also sums up the attitude of an approving audience in his final speech: "You have worked a miracle with your talent, your love, your will, your wit; I don't know whether to say with your womanly qualities or your maternal ones" (89). Carlota's closing rejoinder fixes the basic idea of the play: "Womanly or maternal — it's all one and the same" (89).

One curious facet of this play is the rather practical, nonsentimental approach to marriage. While Carlota and Félix are fond of each other, both confess in word and action that love was not a primary motive in their marriage. Carlota had desperately wanted a home — especially because she had lacked one as a child — and Félix was able to provide it. For Carlota, work in an office was only a temporary measure until a man could provide a home for her. Although a strong, accomplishing woman, Carlota has no feminist inclinations. Félix, likewise, makes clear his position vis-à-vis Carlota: "I don't know how to tell you that I love you. At my age it would be ridiculous to talk of exaltations and raptures. Besides, it probably wouldn't be so!" (32).

In *Mistress of the House*, Martínez Sierra also touches on a theme that figures rather prominently in the feminist essays written years later. Carlota voices basic advice for her stepchildren later given in the feminist essays: she insists on proper diet, rest, simple attire, and cleanliness. The feminist essays particularly stress simple health habits and much soap and water. Such were the Martínez Sierras' simple solutions for bodily ills. Their similarly uncomplicated prescription for mental health was hard work.

CHAPTER 5

Maternal Nuns in Dramas of Renunciation and Revolution

BECAUSE of a generally optimistic and frequently sentimental portrayal of life, Martínez Sierra has not been considered a revolutionary dramatist — or even a social critic, for that matter.[1] His plays featuring religious figures, however — *Cradle Song* (1911), *Lily Among Thorns* (1911), *The Shepherds* (1913), *The Kingdom of God* (1915) and *Holy Night* (1916) — exalt the virtues of Christian charity and self-sacrifice at the same time that they criticize the existing social, religious, and political order. The revolution gently recommended in these plays is essentially a spiritual one involving a return to the universal fundamental of fraternal love. The thrust is consistently humane and vital rather than narrowly religious.

The nuns chosen by Martínez Sierra to convey the message of human charity are, first and foremost, human beings. They suffer, fear, cry, dream and, on occasion, lick cookie pots and stick out their tongues in pique. Despite their human qualities and limitations, these nuns symbolize distilled and sometimes idealized maternity. The selfless dedication shown by these women also functions as a metaphor for the human ideal of Christian charity. Not happy as contemplatives, they seek activity and involvement with living things and need to nurture, be it abandoned child, ailing invalid, hardened sinner, or wounded animal.

María Martínez Sierra, probably the architect of the plays dealt with in this chapter, was educated in a convent. In preparation for the writing of *The Kingdom of God*, her favorite play, she lived for a while in a convent with her sister, a nun serving in a charitable order. Moreover, the message of Christian charity advocated in these plays bears direct relationship to the Socialist one espoused by María. It is unlikely that Gregorio, who early rejected formal religion, would have elected to write about nuns; and despite the fertile

107

imagination attributed to him by María, he would hardly have possessed such insight into the feminine psyche. The nuns of *Cradle Song,* in particular, suggest a painting from real life.

I Cradle Song

Illustrative of Martínez Sierra's ideas as well as his theatrical technique is his masterpiece, *Cradle Song.* Rather than develop a conflict or move toward any climax, this play reveals two moments of convent life as it explores feminine personality. The first act shows several novices celebrating the saint's day of their Mother Superior. A caged bird delivered as a gift allows the novices to reveal their feelings about seclusion in their own convent cage. Later, another object is placed in the convent's revolving turnshelf: a baby abandoned by its mother with a note imploring the nuns to care for this "child of sin" with their virginal hands. The convent doctor adopts the child, thereby solving the legal problem and then entrusts her to the sisters for education. Sister Juana, a novice experienced in child care, tends to the infant's needs and, as the first act ends, plays happily with her tiny charge.

In the second act, eighteen years have elapsed, and the child Teresa, true to the heritage of her blood, is a lively, high-spirited girl with no wish to remain in the convent, despite her deep love for her mothers. She has fallen in love and will marry soon. Although the nuns prepare Teresa's trousseau and share their daughter's joy, they dread the void that awaits them. After Teresa's departure, the nuns attempt to suppress their pain as they file resolutely into the chapel for services. Sister Juana, however, who more than anyone else has been Teresa's special mother, is unable to control her feelings, and as the curtain falls, she is left alone, weeping inconsolably.

Besides stressing throughout his works that women need not give birth physically in order to be excellent mothers, Martínez Sierra utilizes in the plays involving nuns the virgin-mother dichotomy, a paradox prevalent in religion and literature.

As in *Mistress of the House,* there is a strong equating of femininity with maternity. Women, Martínez Sierra insists, are essentially mothers, and when unable to express this basic facet of their personalities, they become frustrated and unhappy; sometimes they even suffer physical or emotional illnesses. In addition, Martínez Sierra suggests — even before Freud made such ideas fashionable — that there is something unnatural and unhealthy about the rejection of all physical expression. When the doctor makes his regular visit to the convent, he finds several symptoms of frustration and latent psychosomatic disturbance. Sister María Consolación, who sometimes complains that a viper gnaws at her vitals, now insists that she has a frog in her throat; (the viper suggests the sexual sin of the Garden of Eden, and the frog has long been a symbol of lust[2]). Marcela, reacting to the gift of the canary to the Mother Superior, opens the cage and urges the bird to fly away; Sister María Jesús, making the symbolic allusion to the convent quite clear, says that the bird chooses to remain caged just like the nuns; Sister Marcela calls the bird foolish for not electing freedom and wishes she could fly over the wall. Sister Sagrario has a recurring dream of flight; Sister María Jesús, eighteen years old, falls asleep in the choir, sighs constantly, has no appetite, and cries without provocation. After lifting this young novice's veil and commenting irreverently on the good taste the Lord has shown in this bride, the doctor prescribes an earthly spouse. When she protests that she has already taken preliminary vows which she proposes to keep, the doctor prescribes an alternate and standard remedy for frustration: exercise and cold showers.[3] Walter Starkie errs when he writes of the nuns in Act 1: "We are admitted to their happy, serene life."[4]

It is through Sister Juana of the Cross that Martínez Sierra combines what is ideal as well as real about the maternal instinct. In subtly suggesting a parallel between Sister Juana and the Virgin Mary, he idealizes Juana as he humanizes the Virgin: in a delicate way, he suggests that Juana is the incarnation of Mary, just as Mary must have been very much like Juana. Sister Juana speaks of how the Virgin washed the baby Jesus' garments in a brook. When she subsequently relates how she washed the clothes of her younger brothers and sisters in a similar fashion, she establishes a relationship between the two virginal mothers, one remote and the other immediate.

Although saddened by separation from her family, Sister Juana is comforted by memories of having played a maternal role with her younger brothers and sisters. Her realistic and maternal orientation even manifests itself in her relationship with God. Rather than visualize Christ in the abstract as a force for good or, more concretely, as the heavenly father, Sister Juana sees God as the child Jesus. It is neither the suffering, ethereal figure on the cross nor the comforting, powerful father that inspires her devotion, but rather Jesus, the helpless baby. She even imagines that the Lord comes to her as an infant in Holy Communion. In the mystic tradition,[5] Juana feels God's presence acutely. Here, however, there is a reversal of roles: while St. John of the Cross and St. Teresa felt themselves enveloped and protected in the arms of their Lord, Sister Juana imagines that she herself maternally envelops and protects the infant Jesus: "Whenever I take communion I try to think I am receiving our Lord as a little child, and I take and press Him like this to my heart, and then it seems to me that He is so little and so helpless that He can't refuse me anything. And then I think that He is crying, and I pray to the Virgin to come and help me quiet Him. And if I wasn't ashamed, because I know you would all laugh at me, I'd croon to Him then and rock Him to sleep, and sing Him baby songs."[6]

Martínez Sierra frequently expresses positive and negative examples through opposing characters. If Sister Juana personifies what is good about the maternal instinct, the Vicaress represents the absence of this quality essential to femininity. Her manner is the reverse of the kindly one shown by the Mother Superior and by Sister Juana, both of whom nurture by instinct and are happy in the expressions of their maternity. Much like the unattractive, unmaternal woman frequently portrayed in other works, she is a negative example of womanhood. Somewhat like Lorca's Bernarda Alba in her rigid attention to rule and appearance, she overlooks the simple irony that in order to receive love one must give it. The Vicaress is really the only openly discordant, slightly embittered voice in the play.[7] Unlike *Yerma*, a play that Lorca wrote on the subject of the maternal instinct, the thrust of *Cradle Song* is communal in that the theme is diffused in various characters. Lorca's play, on the other hand, is centripetal, intense, and violent in exploring the maternal force principally through one archetypal character. In both plays the characters develop only in relationship to the theme of maternal instinct.[8]

The Interlude between the acts lyrically summarizes *Cradle Song*'s statement regarding the enormously important role of the maternal instinct in every facet of life. This force functions, Martínez Sierra affirms, in every relationship involving women, whether they be lovers, friends, sisters, or mothers.

The author's subtle implication in Act 2 is that the novices, now nuns, have maintained equilibrium through maternal expression toward Teresa. Given the suggestion of their frustration in the first act, these nuns might have lost mental and physical balance in an absurd world of women without children — or at least become embittered, as has the Vicaress.

Because Martínez Sierra insisted so strongly on the importance of expressing the maternal instinct, he is almost compelled to explain how the older nuns in this cloistered convent have survived prior to the arrival of Teresa. The Mother Superior and the Mistress of Novices "mother" the new members of the community. Toward the end of Act 1, the Mistress of Novices provides an explanation for the rest of the nuns as she speaks in favor of keeping the abandoned child: "Suppose, your reverences, it hadn't been a little girl, but . . . I don't know — some poor animal, a dog, a cat, or a dove, like the one which flew in here trying to get away from those butchers at the pigeon traps. Wouldn't we have taken it in? Wouldn't we have cared for it? And wouldn't it have lived happy forever afterward in its cage? And how can we do less for a creature with a soul than for a bird?" (29).

While some may see *Cradle Song* as the sweet expression of idealized and pure maternal love, it is, in addition, a drama of feminine frustration and, in some cases, of forced rather than voluntary renunciation of self. Although the motivations of the women in coming to the convent are not explored, the implication is that they came out of financial need and family or social pressure rather than an authentic religious vocation. In this sense, these women are like Teresa and her mother, victims of a social system that tended to channel women to the home, the convent, or the brothel. Although the Martínez Sierras recommend no solution to the various problems alluded to in this play, they certainly suggest that the convent is not a happy solution for economic or social ills.

II   Lily Among Thorns

A few months after the enormously successful opening of *Cradle Song*, Martínez Sierra presented *Lirio entre espinas (Lily Among Thorns*, 1911), a play of similar theme and structure in which the situation is reversed. In *Cradle Song*, an infant of worldly — even "sinful" — origin comes by chance or miracle to a group of women who sorely need her. Teresa, a victim of society's ills, is mothered by virgins in a spiritual sanctuary. She provides a physical and emotional outlet and thereby saves the nuns as much as they save her. In *Lily Among Thorns*, the scene is a house of prostitution into which a nun stumbles — again by chance or divine plan — at a time of need. This "lily" briefly provides the "thorns" with the maternal care and spiritual orientation needed in a moment of crisis.

Lily Among Thorns combines elements of fantasy and reality as it recalls a moment of recent Spanish history: Barcelona's "Tragic Week" of 1909. During these bloody days, opposition to military service in Morocco had sparked a general strike, the burning of convents and churches, riots in the streets and general chaos. The curtain on this one-act play goes up to reveal — as had *Cradle Song* — a house inhabited entirely by women. This time, however, the inhabitants are prostitutes rather than nuns. One of the girls is dancing on the table as her "sisters" and two clients, Carlos and Agustín, offer encouragement. The sounds of laughter and hand clapping merge with the noises of machine-gun fire from the street. In much of his work and in all of the plays in this chapter, Martínez Sierra illustrates an affinity for dichotomies. Here, the raw vitality of the brothel and its affirmation of life are juxtaposed with destruction and the threat of extinction in the streets. Presiding over this ambivalent scene with what the author describes as "almost maternal benevolence," is Tomasa, the madam, an ironic parallel of the Mother Superior in *Cradle Song.*

Disgusted by the lack of concern that the house clients, Carlos and Agustín, show in this moment of national crisis, Lulu, a forerunner of the feminist heroine, calls the men "idiots."[9] She wishes she were a man so she could fight for her beliefs. The men reply good-naturedly that they are here to defend the women, for as soon as the Anarchists have burned all the convents they will surely come to destroy this "house of pleasure." A surprised Tomasa retorts that her establishment does no harm to anyone. Unlike the convents, she reasons with some pride, this house pays taxes (9). Carlos then explains the Anarchists' point of view: "But you, my darlings, are luxury objects; the privilege of the infamous bourgeoisie who pay for your charms with the sweat of the poor and exploited" (9). Agustín labels Tomasa a Socialist when she suggests that the house could provide free services for the poor and raise the prices for the rich (9–10). Lulu then, in a comment reminiscent of Socialist María Martínez Sierra, interjects: "In the world there are only two forces: money and hunger. With the money of everyone, everyone eats. Well, I say they [the rich] should give it willingly or we should take it away from them" (10).

Lulu desperately wants to join in the revolutionary action in the streets and finally convinces Agustín to accompany her. When Tomasa asks in surprise where they are going on such a night, Agustín wearily suggests that they are seeking a heroic death. Lulu bitterly affirms an awareness of the limited options open to women, as she replies to Tomasa: "You and I won't be so lucky. We have to die of disgust, fever, or a falling ceiling tile" (23). As Agustín and Lulu depart, the street fighting increases. The sound of footsteps is heard very shortly on the stairs, and the group huddles together for protection, fearing the entry of an angry Anarchist. At the moment of most tension, the door opens to reveal a nun, Sister Teresa, a victim of the turmoil.[10] Her convent has been burned, and, in the ensuing confusion, she seeks refuge at any door.

The situation of this play is novel and daring; moreover, when Sister Teresa rather than the expected revolutionary appears at the door, the author has captured the attention of his audience. He fails to capitalize on his advantage, however, and the play soon loses compression. Rather than emphasize the drama of the moment or the pathos of the situation, the author allows Sister Teresa and the men to talk at cross-purposes as he employs some humor of questionable taste, unusual for him.[11] At this point, Agustín bursts in carrying a bleeding and unconscious Lulu. Although before their arrival Sister Teresa was uncomfortable and preferred the uncertainty of the streets, she now knows that she is needed. Putting all personal considerations aside, she ministers to Lulu's wounds and makes her comfortable. When she regains consciousness, Lulu speaks of the revolution as beautiful: "It is wonderful to see. It makes you want to climb up on anything and shout to them that they are right. Because they are right. *(To the nun)* Isn't that so, ma'am?" (45). When Sister Teresa lowers her eyes and responds only "God knows . . .", Lulu continues: "Yes, they are right. In the world, there shouldn't be poor people or rich people. Everyone should be happy. *(With feverish emotion)* Everyone should be equal" (45).

Sister Teresa then turns her attentions to Ricardito, a young man of limited intelligence who frequents the house. Although the prostitutes make fun of him, Sister Teresa treats Ricardito tenderly, tells him she loves him, and invites him to go home with her. There, she promises, there are others like him, and, she explains: "There we would take care of you and you would learn to be good, to read, to pray. You would learn a trade, and then you would be a productive man and earn your living. What do you say?" (49). In this scene, Martínez Sierra establishes Sister Teresa as a member not of a contemplative order — as was the case in *Cradle Song* — but of a charitable one that ministers to the less fortunate members of society.

After having charmed Ricardito completely Teresa, very much like Carlota of *Mistress of the House*, turns her attentions to other problems. Lulu has become delirious, but Sister Teresa, progressively calmer as she responds to the needs of those around her, confidently cares for the girl. A few moments later, Tomasa reports an apparent miracle wrought by the nun with Lulu: "She has saintly hands. I don't know what she did, but the fact is that [Lulu] stopped screaming immediately and is calm now; she only sighs a little. . . . She gave her a little medicine and sat at the head of the bed, took her prayer book out, and says that she is going to spend the night watching over her" (53). Inspired by this act of charity for a total stranger, the prostitutes abandon their companions in the salon to join Sister Teresa in prayer. Tomasa's final words illustrate a brand of "female chauvinism" characteristic of Martínez Sierra: "Woman can descend to the depths, but she always has her religion, because she is a woman and because she has been reared properly, not like these shameless men — not even the devil knows what to do with them" (58). As the curtain falls, the stage is bare, and one hears only the chorus of female voices — prostitutes and nun — as they say the rosary together in a poignant and effective ending to an uneven play.

In *Lily Among Thorns*, actual revolution forms a background for the exaltation of women and their natural maternal virtues. This one play involves a real rather than a symbolic revolution, and Lulu expresses the militant desire for a more just world, and a willingness to die for her beliefs. Sister Teresa, on the other hand, has given up all rights to assert herself. She is, nevertheless, a model for the spiritual and social revolution favored by the Martínez Sierras. Were everyone like Sister Teresa, the revolt of the streets would be quite unnecessary.

III   The Kingdom of God

Of the three plays featuring maternal nuns, *El reino de Dios (The Kingdom of God,* 1915) is the one that most accentuates the theme of personal renunciation for the social good. Its philosophy, if generally adopted, would bring the "kingdom of God" to earth. Unlike *Cradle Song,* this play provides a tour de force acting role in Sister Gracia, the figure who provides unity to the episodic drama. Like *Cradle Song,* it reveals decisive moments of feminine life. Act 1 presents Sister Gracia, as a gay, hopeful nineteen-year-old postulant who cares for aging and destitute men. In Act 2, ten years have elapsed and at twenty-nine, she is tired, discouraged, and exposed to temptation as she works in a hospital for unwed mothers. Act 3 shows her as a woman of seventy, wisely and tenderly mothering a group of orphaned and abandoned children.[12]

Although none of the plays featuring nuns focuses on the religious life as such, there is in *Cradle Song* an implied criticism of the cloister, for Martínez Sierra firmly believed that women needed active involvement with people. In *The Kingdom of God,* Sister Gracia is neither a cloistered nun nor does she take perpetual vows. As a Sister of Charity she takes vows only yearly. Moreover, her vocation is authentic, for as a member of a wealthy family, she came to the order freely, not out of economic necessity. Her mother, an uncomprehending bourgeois woman, fails to understand how her daughter can choose to move among the unclean or uncultured. As Sister Gracia explains why she must give not only of her possessions but of herself, she establishes early in the play the renunciation motif:

Give alms! No . . . no . . . oh, no! Where's the good in giving away a little of what you have too much of . . . and keeping the rest . . . and not caring . . . spending money amusing oneself . . . while they have so much to endure . . . and you do nothing for them, nothing at all? . . . For misery is wickedness and want is a crime . . . because God gave His world to us all alike . . . and our daily bread. And if His children starve and are homeless . . . that's a crime, yes, a crime. And the man who keeps more than he needs robs the man who's in need. Turn away your eyes when your brother is dying . . . and you're an accomplice in his death . . . . I've nothing to give but my happiness . . . so I want to give that, you see, to those that have none.[13]

Precisely because Sister Gracia chooses to become a nun as well as remain one, her personal sacrifice is all the more admirable. In an important scene of Act 2, her renunciation is tested at a vulnerable moment: the doctor who attends the women and children in the maternity hospital declares his love for her. He reminds her that she may allow her vows to lapse and marry him with no feeling of failure. Despite her fatigue and even a feeling that she has momentarily lost contact with God, Sister Gracia conquers temptation and opts for the common good over personal happiness.

Near the end of her life, Sister Gracia, now seventy, cares for orphan boys. In a key scene somewhat reminiscent of *Lily Among Thorns*, the children, displeased with their food, threaten revolt. The leader tells Sister Gracia that there can be no God, because He would not allow the world to be so unjust. Sister Gracia's reply fixes the ideal of Christian charity and brotherhood that lies at the heart of the Martínez Sierra revolution:

God does not think this [injustice] is right. Men break His laws. He made them brothers. Is it His fault if they turn wolves and devour each other? God does not think it right that His children go hungry . . . and the innocent are not ever disgraced in His eyes. It is by no will of His that some are poor and neglected while some are set up in pride. For God is Love and He loves us all, and to each one He gives a share in heaven and in this earth. . . . God does not smile upon the injustice of this world. He endures it . . . for how long? . . . ah, that we do not know. But He does not think it right" (101).

Convinced by Sister Gracia's message and example, the boys return, chastened, to their meager soup. She admonishes them to remember that children are the hope of the world and that their responsibility is to see that hunger, injustice, and poverty are eradicated. "My sons," she implores them, "promise me that when you are men you'll try to bring these things to pass . . . that you'll help to build on earth the Kingdom of God" (102).

IV Holy Night

The three plays involving maternal nuns evince a progression from involuntary to voluntary renunciation of the world; from dedication to one individual — Teresa, of *Cradle Song* — to a dedication to all society in *The Kingdom of God*. Although *Navidad (Holy*

Night, 1916), subtitled "A Miracle Play," features no nun, the Virgin Mary performs a similar function in a play identical in ideological thrust. *Holy Night* carries the renunciation theme to its limit as it portrays the woman chosen by God to be His mother — and hence the symbolic mother of mankind — performing the ultimate renunciation: she delivers her divine Child to the needy. After this play, a return to the theme of maternal renunciation would have been anticlimactic. Perhaps for this reason *Holy Night* is the final play in the cycle.

As the curtain goes up on *Holy Night,* it is Christmas Eve. In the interior of a Gothic cathedral resplendent with candles, the celebrant of midnight Mass places the image of the Christ Child in an altar nativity scene. Close to the baby, the Virgin is seated on a throne surrounded by angels and shepherds. After the faithful leave the church, the Virgin rises, takes her child, and, accompanied by a group of angels and saints, goes out into the night to visit the poor, the hungry, the afflicted. In this humanistic and modern allegory,[14] St. Francis of Assisi guides the Virgin and informs a gathering throng of curious thieves, drunkards, and prostitutes that the Holy Mother has come particularly in search of them. When they react in disbelief, St. Francis reminds them that Jesus too befriended sinners, the poor, the ignorant, the hungry, the exploited, and the oppressed.

A member of the crowd dressed in ragged garments recognizes the Virgin and, enraptured, throws himself at her feet. The crowd identifies him as Don Manuel, "the mad priest" who frequents the taverns to aid the discouraged. He preaches in the streets, has built a shelter for prostitutes, begs food for the hungry, and shares all he has with the poor. Don Manuel is, in fact, a modern-day Christ figure. His name Manuel (Emmanuel) suggests his role, and the parallel of his actions with those of Jesus — also an outcast of society — reinforces the identity. He is no longer a priest, explains one, because a grateful recipient of his kindness kissed him as he walked with the bishop.[15]

A sharp contrast to Don Manuel, whom the bishop has judged unfit to be a priest, is the sacristan. Having discovered the disappearance of the costly images from the church, he comes to this poor section of Madrid, believing that they have been stolen. St. Francis assures the sacristan that the Virgin has come of her own free will in search of those in need of her Son. The sacristan is unable to understand how the Virgin can have intentionally abandoned a great cathedral to visit the poorest section of Madrid. St. Francis explains that she seeks neither gold nor frankincense, but myrrh: "Myrrh is bitter . . . myrrh is hunger and cold . . . is helplessness and desolation . . . is poverty and ignorance. . . . The bitterness of the world *(pointing to the crowd)* is here. . . ."[16] Uncomprehending, the sacristan continues to implore the Virgin to return so that the church may function normally on Christmas Day. His concern with the appearance of the statues in the church rather than with the presence of the Holy Spirit underscores his preoccupation (and by extension the preoccupation of the Church and the wealthy) with the Virgin and Child as possessions rather than forces of love and hope.

On this miraculous night the Virgin deliberately renounces worldly position, honor, and comfort to befriend the poor, the hopeless, and the destitute. In a supreme gesture of love, she delivers her only Child to the ragged multitude. Don Manuel, who with the Virgin personifies the spirit of true Christian charity, admonishes the crowd to keep the Christ Child with them always (53). The sacristan, still failing to understand the spiritual message of the Virgin's gesture, implores her once more to return with him. St. Francis instructs the sacristan to return to the church, open the doors, and ring the bells, "for whosoever shall sincerely come in search of the Child and His mother will surely find them" (54). In the final scene of *Holy Night*, the Virgin and St. Francis pray together for the persecuted and the miserable as the curtain slowly descends.

In several ways, *Holy Night* is a more symbolic, more theological version of *The Kingdom of God*. In the latter play, Sister Gracia, a humanized "Holy Mother," ministers to the world's most needy as she renounces the comfort of home and family. In *Holy Night*, the Virgin makes the ultimate gesture of maternal renunciation as she delivers her divine and only child to the poor. Martínez Sierra suggests that human selfishness has obscured the meaning of Christ's birth. Beneath the false trappings imposed by a materialistic power structure, however, Jesus and his mother continue to set examples of sacrifice, humility, and love. They, like the nuns of the other plays, not only befriend outcasts of society, but reject the values of — and association with — a selfish and insensitive Establishment.[17] In this sense all of these figures, like Jesus himself, are

revolutionaries. On a hopeful note *Holy Night* implies, in its contemporary setting, that the miracle of two thousand years ago remains within grasp through a return to the simple traditions of
brotherhood and love.[18]

CHAPTER 6

The Feminist Heroines: Women in Search of Equality

THE feminist movement has been an important force in the Scandinavian countries, in the United States, England, France, Germany, and the Communist countries. In Spain, on the contrary, several factors (predominantly Moorish and Roman Catholic) have retarded its development. For the woman to consider the fate that tradition reserved for her if she endangered the family's honor by free association with men could be enough to deter her from such behavior. Since the Spanish woman in the early twentieth century tended to follow the precepts established by Fray Luis de León in his sixteenth-century work, *La perfecta casada (The Perfect Wife*, 1583), Martínez Sierra's ideas must have seemed revolutionary indeed.

Martínez Sierra's feminist heroine will lift no eyebrows now as she did between 1910 and 1930, for she represents approximately what the nonviolent, middle-of-the-road feminists say all over the world: that a woman has much to contribute outside the home and that domestic tasks, far from exhausting her powers, do not begin to tap her resources. This heroine, a little left of center for the 1970's in her insistence that women be equals with men not only in rights but in responsibilities as well, does align herself with the right in the sense that she in no way rejects femininity or the role of wife and mother.

Although the word "feminism" never appears in their plays, the Martínez Sierras illustrate in certain works their published definition of the term: "Feminism proposes that women enjoy fulfilling lives, which is to say that they should have the same rights and the same responsibilities as men; that they should share in the government of the world since together they populate it; that in perfect collaboration they try to make each other happy and to make the human species better. Both men and women should enjoy a serene

120

life, founded on mutual tolerance between equal partners, not on the degrading submission of the weaker to the stronger. Feminism is opposed to the selfish tyranny of the person who believes that he (or she) is more important."[1] The independent women they promote are feminists only in the sense that they believe in equality of opportunity and seek actively to participate in and contribute to the world outside the home. Never members of an organization to fight for women's rights, these women study, work, or are active because of an inner need, blazing a path for other women more out of instinct than social conscience. In this sense, they are peculiarly Spanish, for they are more passionate than organized, more individual than group-oriented.

The feminist heroines follow, in general, the suggestions outlined in the essays on women. Of particular importance is the moral, economic, and social equality of the sexes. Because Martínez Sierra believed that the ultimate expression of femininity was maternity, the heroines tend to nurture, whether the object nurtured be child (usually not her own), husband, relative, bird, animal, or plant. Unlike the recipe-swapping, scatterbrained, childlike caricature of the dependent and exclusively domestic homebody, the ideal woman Martínez Sierra portrayed is intelligent, educated, independent, active, gently aggressive, and always Spanish. As a foil for the modern, career-oriented woman, Martínez Sierra frequently utilized a conservative older woman, often the protagonist's mother, as the negative example of what women become when forced to stagnate in the home.

If married, this active heroine believes that all decisions affecting the family should be made jointly by husband and wife. She also feels a responsibility to assist in maintaining the home, economically as well as ideologically. Indeed, she finds that life is most rewarding when she uses her capabilities and energies constructively. The exclusively domestic woman of the past might have taken out frustrations on husband and children (as in the case of the conservative mother or the Vicaress of *Cradle Song*), destroying thereby the emotional unity and tranquility of the family. The feminist heroine, on the other hand, asserts herself and joyfully contributes her energies through work accomplished either in the home (writing, for example) or outside of it. Ideally she and her husband work together, frequently as doctors or writers.

Morally, Martínez Sierra finds the human ideal reflected in the standards traditionally set for woman. They would not, for example, grant woman the right some men take of bending the rules. The double standard, based on the idea that "boys will be boys," establishes a more flexible rule for men while requiring that women adhere to a stricter one. In a sense, Martínez Sierra sees women as morally and spiritually superior to men, for they have been much more successful in controlling human appetites of all kinds. A more realistic solution, perhaps, is that men, having established and policed moral standards, overlook transgressions among their own but require stricter compliance in the case of women. As previously stated, absolute equality is a basic tenet of Martínez Sierra's feminism.

Ignoring such negative and theoretically feminine traits as vanity, jealousy, emotionalism, inconstancy, and so on, the Martínez Sierras strongly emphasize the positive feminine qualities to show the independent Spanish woman as the epitome of feminine virtue. They suggest that woman's sensitivity, intuition, sympathy, understanding, gentleness, and physical appeal make her especially well-equipped for careers that involve personal contact and insist that nondomestic occupations, far from being prejudicial, enrich and refresh her for the challenge of husband and children. While the Martínez Sierra heroine is no *femme fatale*, the authors did seem to sanction the use of feminine wiles (and hence the exploitation of masculine vulnerability to these tactics) as perfectly fair and ethical weapons for a woman to employ in accomplishing her goals. Perhaps this low-key, somewhat traditional approach to liberation accounts for the fact that this fictional feminist did not offend or shock in an environment rather hostile to the idea of women's rights. The model liberated woman in the Martínez Sierra plays, portrayed so convincingly by Catalina Bárcena for many years, is intelligent but not pedantic, independent but not rejecting, pretty but not vampish, positive but not domineering, virtuous but not prudish, ambitious but not pushy, strong but not overbearing. She is, in a word abhorred by "gut" feminists, feminine. Since the spotlight in these plays focuses on women and their victories (yes, they almost always have their way), the men seem weak and vacillating.[2]

The plays illustrating the ideas the Martínez Sierras held about women tend to present colorful, strong heroines and pallid, ultimately retiring men. Perhaps the least retiring and most modern of the male characters is Emilio, of *Seamos felices (Let's Be Happy,*

1929), who faces a most determined heroine in Fernanda. The title is significantly in the plural, for Fernanda seeks happiness and fulfillment in union rather than in competition with her husband. She feels that both husband and wife should work and divide life's responsibilities; work for her implies sharing, not rivalry.

In the early scenes of *Let's Be Happy*, Fernanda lives with her mother, who, in the old Spanish tradition, feels that a well-reared young lady does no work outside her own home. Fernanda, whose talents center on the piano, dreams of a concert career. Her mother values her accomplishments for a more domestic purpose, such as playing to soothe a harassed husband and entertaining the many children that will certainly come. Although Fernanda resolves the conflict with her mother when she marries Emilio, she soon encounters a more serious problem. She receives an offer to make a well-paid concert tour that will also include all traveling expenses for herself and Emilio. Since her husband has financial difficulties, she feels the offer comes from heaven and gives her an opportunity to contribute materially to the marriage. When Emilio refuses to consent (and in those days his written consent was legally necessary), Fernanda, in astonishment at his attitude, appeals to his common sense for an honest interpretation of their marriage contract: "But I'm your wife! Don't you remember what the priest told you? 'To help each other.' To help each other, huh? If you just knew how I enjoy spending the money you earn! Why should it give you any less pleasure to spend the money that I earn?"[3]

While Emilio is modern and enlightened, his liberality has limitations which do not include being supported by a wife, even on a temporary basis. Fernanda asks him if he could be content to renounce all plans for a career just to love, and be adored by, his wife. Emilio automatically responds, "But that's different! I'm a man!"[4], and thus he activates the feminist. Fernanda fairly sputters in her disbelief: "Can it be you . . . who has said that? You, such a modern man . . . have been capable of saying . . . of saying . . . of thinking . . . that *(She smiles)* aberration *(Repeating)* 'I am a man' . . . that is to say, I am a . . . supernatural being . . . the only one of the couple that you and I form that has a right to life? That's a joke!"[5] By recourse to feminine wiles, Fernanda circumvents Emilio's objections and is ultimately successful in her project.

Fernanda, in her assertive behavior, was the product of early twentieth-century Spain, a country slowly awakening to the changes of the modern world. The intellectuals of the Generation of '98 had, in general, favored breaking away from traditional molds, and women, seeing their opportunities, sought more rights in the shifting society. Most of all, these Spanish feminists wanted to express themselves outside the home. They wanted to use their abilities in a market which would not ridicule them or discriminate because of sex. They believed that the exclusion, of women, by law or by tradition, from active participation in society was wasteful, for it meant ignoring approximately half of the nation's talent. If only one person were kept from making a beneficial contribution, there would be a loss, while there could be no possible gain in blanket exclusion of thousands of persons whose capabilities were largely unknown but potentially important.

In 1919, when *Cada uno y su vida (To Each His Own)* was performed, a few Spanish women were entering universities to prepare themselves for careers. Irene, the main character, illustrates and indirectly champions this cultural change. The daughter of a laundress, Irene is a medical student who works for a doctor to support herself. The doctor's wife, Carolina, considers Irene odd and unfeminine for trying to enter a profession generally considered appropriate only for men. The physician points out that Irene's academic record far surpasses in excellence that of their medical student son, Carlos, who, incidentally, gradually develops more than a casual interest in Irene. In the face of Carolina's coldness, Irene is long-suffering without ever becoming subservient. Though Irene is extremely ambitious, she would never consider recourse to marriage either to further her career or to acquire status or comfort. When she and Carlos become more involved, she attempts to end the relationship, for she realizes that not only is she breaking the unwritten law that a woman's place is in the home but that she is straining another which dictates that marriage partners should come from similar social backgrounds. Carlos needs Irene, however, and the play ends with the implication that they will resolve together the problems that arise.

In *To Each His Own*, several frequently repeated ideas converge. Irene is a typical Martínez Sierra feminist heroine in the following ways: not only are her capabilities equal to those of the man opposite her, they are superior; she, as a woman, is shown to be better equipped temperamentally and intellectually for certain careers (medicine in this case) than the man; she displays nobility of character; she works and feels that marriage is not an obstacle to her career or happiness but is simply another necessary and desirable goal; she will work with her husband after marriage.

The ideal arrangement, the Martínez Sierras repeatedly assert, is for husband and wife to work together as Irene and Carlos will in medicine. That the woman was happier and the marriage more stable when husband and wife shared responsibilities, and especially when they worked together, was an idea portrayed repeatedly not only in the theater of this writing team, but in the essays, novels, and poetry as well. The importance of professional partnership was not just something Gregorio and María wrote about; they lived it. Perhaps this factor accounts for the frequency with which the theme appears.

In addition to Irene of *To Each His Own,* Carolina's daughter, Luz, is a Spanish feminist in the making. She reads biology books as a pastime and dreams of a career in medicine. In one scene, the traditionalist attitudes of the mother appear ridiculous in comparison to those of the career-minded young woman.

CAROLINA: What did Irene bring you?
LUZ: *(a little shocked)* A book.
CAROLINA: A novel!
LUZ: No.
CAROLINA: In English. What does this mean, "biology"?
LUZ: Biology . . . the science of life.
CAROLINA: And what do you read that for?
LUZ: To learn, mother.
CAROLINA: To learn about the science of life? Can it be that you want to be a doctor, too? *(She looks at her daughter disapprovingly.)*
LUZ: If only I can, mother! *(with timid passion)* A doctor or anything, but just have a career!
CAROLINA: Don't be silly! The only decent career for a woman is marriage . . . a socially advantageous marriage![6]

Carolina represents the traditionalist point of view that a woman's place is in the home and that education and intellectual stimulation are neither desirable nor appropriate for her. The mother of grown children in these plays is, with few exceptions, rigid and antiintellectual in her views on what constitutes propriety for women. A spokesman for tradition,[7] she in no way relates to the expression of the maternal instinct, a theme treated with great tenderness and respect in many plays.[8]

María Luisa, of *El corazón ciego* (*The Blind Heart*, 1919), has both the characteristic conservative mother and the typical preoccupation of the Martínez Sierra feminist: equality of the sexes, moral as well as professional. After a youthful indiscretion on the part of María Luisa, her mother anxiously encourages her to accept the proposal of Antonio, a penniless young man initially attracted to her money. María Luisa despises the thought that to acquire respectability she has only to marry. Antonio, whom she ultimately does marry, has made mistakes too but believes that his are unimportant because he is a man. In referring to their past peccadillos, Antonio utters those fighting words, "I'm a man! It's different!" and triggers a feminist response. One must imagine the anger, frustration, and righteous indignation of María Luisa's brief but significant retort: "It's the same!"[9]

After their marriage, María Luisa and Antonio move to Tangier where Antonio, unwilling to accept assistance from his wife's family, works hard to support them both. Because he does not want his wife to work, María Luisa, always eager to learn, finds an outlet for some of her energy in the study of Arabic. Although Sidi Mohamet, her tutor, presents an attractive idyl of the silent, submissive, oriental wife, María Luisa's outlook remains decidedly occidental in her insistence on shared responsibilities: "I am very proud! I don't want, as Mohamet says, to be the garden of the tired man; I want to share in the planting and share in the harvest."[10] At the play's end, a business venture in which both husband and wife participate, sets the marriage on a successful course.

A play with a solution similar to the one in *The Blind Heart* is *Amanecer* (*Dawn*, 1919). In the first act, Carmen, the main character, is a typical frivolous debutante. The flight of her father after embezzling some funds left in his keeping considerably alters her philosophy of life, and she goes to work to support herself and her mother. When Mariano, the young man she thinks she loves, leaves for Africa to seek his fortune, she is dejected and in his absence finds it expedient to marry Julián, her wealthy employer. Believing that she has sold herself, Carmen at first feels martyred and continues to long for Mariano. When he returns from Africa, however, Carmen sees him in a different light and realizes that what she had thought was love was closer to blind infatuation, for Julián is by far the superior man. Julián suffers a business reverse at this time and kindly assures Carmen that she need not share his poverty. Carmen is almost relieved, for now she may prove her love and loyalty by remaining at his side and, even more important, can be a partner in building the new business. As the curtain falls, Carmen begins to audit the accounts and make notes. Revealing her joy at the prospect of mutual interest and responsibility, she exclaims: "Today my life begins."[11]

El palacio triste (*The Sad Palace*, 1911), a play composed for children's theater, could be interpreted as a Socialist-feminist allegory. Marta, the young princess who fits nicely into the pattern of the liberated woman, left the palace three years ago, at the age of twelve, to search for the meaning of life. Like the other feminist characters, she is courageous and her main defense is action. Marta, a practical girl frustrated with her irrelevant studies in the palace, has a burning desire to earn a living and be independent. Rather than be a parasite, she needs to work, for her pride is in accomplishment. She is proud of her little cottage in the woods, for her labor has built it; the doll that she will buy with her own money will be dearer than the hundreds of dolls she has been given because she will have earned it.

Marta eventually returns to the palace for her mother and brothers so that they may live in the little cottage together, each contributing something to the well-being of the others. At fifteen, Marta is a woman of decision and action who seeks responsibility rather than protection. She epitomizes the Martínez Sierra liberated woman in her search for independence, love, work, freedom, and shared responsibilities.

Rosario, of *Sueño de una de agosto* (*Dream of an August Eve*, 1918) is the best known and the least aggressive of the Martínez Sierra feminists. In fact, she is so gentle and so naive that one wonders if the authors did not create her with tongue in cheek. Whether to classify her as a feminist or a pseudo-feminist is a debatable point. She resents the liberty her three brothers have which allows them to study and to come and go without explanations, but most of all, she resents their right to work and make decisions while she is expected to wait until a man chooses her to shine by his reflected glory. She mimics her brothers as she complains to Doña Barbarita, her grandmother:

You're hearing them. (*Looking around as if her brothers were present.*) "I'll work . . . I'll earn . . . I'll struggle." And what about me? (*Imitating Pepe*)

"Well you, well you'll marry, naturally." *(Getting up, angrily)* You'll get married! In plain language that means you'll let yourself be bought and supported by some little gentleman who is successful. And if I don't get married? *(Imitating Pepe)* "Just pray to God that we get rich and you'll see what a wonderful life you will have." Well, I don't feel like spending my life sponging off anyone! *(Imitating Mario)* "There goes Mario Castellano's sister!" *(Indignant)* How stupid! That's not it, for goodness sake! That's not it! What I need for them to say, if they say anything, is "There goes Rosarito Castellanos. . . . She . . . , she . . . she . . . Yes, sir, she herself, ugly or pretty, dumb or bright, a winner or a loser, but proud of her own life and not of the laurels of any man!"[12]

When a gentleman (the *Aparecido*, the "Stranger") enters Rosario's room in pursuit of a hat blown off by the wind, the authors have a chance to protest comically and gently the injustice of the double standard. If people learn that a man has been in Rosario's room at night, her reputation is ruined while his, if anything, is enhanced.

ROSARIO: If you jump through my window and the world thinks that it is with my consent, your reputation loses nothing. Mine, on the other hand, would be totally lost forever. Do you think that's right?
STRANGER: *(Humbly)* No, ma'm.
ROSARIO: *(Aggressively)* Do you think it's fair that in this society men have all the rights and women all the responsibilities?
STRANGER: *(Warily)* From what you say, I assume that you would like to leap through the window with as much impunity as a man.
ROSARIO: *(Angrily)* No, sir; you are completely mistaken! *(Indignant)* What I want is that the man who leaps through a window be just as dishonored and just as compromised as the woman inside.
STRANGER: Yes . . . that is a point of view. . . .
ROSARIO: A fair and rational one! The only one, really: equal rights, equal responsibilities![13]

At times, *Dream of an August Eve* seems to make gentle fun of the naive Rosario. She thinks she is very enlightened and sincerely aspires to be what she calls "free," but as the Stranger learns after a very few minutes, she is only superficially modern. Her tastes are decidedly old fashioned:

STRANGER: *(Calmly)* It looks like you are a modern woman.
ROSARIO: *(Getting up with great dignity)* Extremely modern!
STRANGER: I have my doubts. Because if it were true, you wouldn't have the patience to read that.[14]

"That" refers to an ultrasentimental novel that Rosario has been reading. The Stranger accuses the author of falsification and of exploiting romance and illusion to sell his books to women. The writer is Rosario's idol, and she defends him as having great insight into the feminine heart. When the Stranger admits that he has a confidence of sorts with the novelist in question and that the latter is looking for a secretary, Rosario, thrilled and excited, makes plans to apply for the position.

Although Rosario has no financial need to work, she longs to accomplish something outside the home for her own stimulation and self-satisfaction. Her nonviolent, responsible feminism is apparent as she muses: "Earn my own living? It's true . . . I don't need to . . . which means that in my family there are men who can support me. . . . *(Pathetically)* And that precisely is the bitterest disappointment, the blackest humiliation of being a woman! I'm tired of being a parasite!"[15]

Dream of an August Eve also suggested the irony of the Spanish woman's situation. While there were no longer any legal barriers to her working, the great weight of tradition was against it, especially if the woman was married. The working girl in the play, the secretary of the Stranger, feels compelled to resign because she is about to get married. When Rosario applies for the opening and the Stranger reveals himself as the admired author, one can almost see the final curtain falling on the perfect Martínez Sierra solution for Rosario: marriage for love, and a career in collaboration with her husband.

Feminine assertion as practiced two generations earlier is outlined by Doña Barbarita, amused by her granddaughter's frustration at the lack of feminine equality:

ROSARIO: You laugh and you don't understand me, because you belong to another century, and in your time you women loved being slaves to men.
DOÑA BARBARITA: My child, the only person who ever liked slavery was the master. What happens is that you [modern women] want to rid yourself of tyranny and we were content just to get even with the tyrant.
ROSARIO: How?
DOÑA BARBARITA: Making his life unbearable. *(Opening a locket with three leaves that she wears on a chain around her neck)* Look! My three masters. My, how they adored me! And how I made them all suffer! *(Smiling satisfied with her memories of marriage)* I made my Ernesto suffer with my jealousy if he ever looked at another woman! And he was a painter! I made Enrique suffer with his own jealousy, premature, but perhaps prophetic, of my Pepe, who was a neighbor of ours and used to wink at me

from the balcony. I made Pepe suffer a posthumous kind of jealousy over Enrique. You women nowadays are more noble but not nearly as happy; you ask for equal rights and give up the sly digs; it's probably more moral, but it certainly isn't as much fun.[16]

Although Estrella, the main character of *Mujer (Woman*, 1924), never works outside her home, she shows spiritual solidarity with feminism in her insistence on moral equality for men and women. A Spanish housewife whose consuming interests are husband and home, Estrella lives a simple, automatic kind of life until she learns that her husband, Gabriel, is involved with another woman. She then begins to examine her feelings about marriage and becomes active rather than passive for the first time in her life. Repelled by the thought that her husband is free to take a mistress while she is expected to accept and forgive, Estrella shows herself to be a woman in search of equality in her marriage when she informs Gabriel that he has no more right to stray than she. He may choose between her and the other woman, but he may not have both. Some months elapse between this confrontation and the second act, which reveals a dramatic change in decor and spirit. Instead of the conventional furniture, decorous Watteau painting, and the rather dull servant in evidence in the first act, we see a bold arrangement of contemporary furniture, an attractively uniformed maid, a painting of a nude, and a sculptured piece of Cupid and Psyche. The atmosphere is seductive, modern, and infinitely more interesting. Estrella goes out in the evening chicly dressed without making explanations and receives flowers from a mysterious source. Gabriel, believing that his wife is seeing another man, is both angry and bewildered. This heroine believes in the validity of marital fidelity and is not seeking sexual license that custom has somehow awarded men, so in reality there is not another man. She simply makes the point that infidelity is painful. She also hopes to awaken her husband's masculine pride and challenge him to win her back. Again, feminine wiles and masculine vulnerability to them are major tactics. After a few more womanly ploys by this feminist unaware, Gabriel returns to the marriage on Estrella's terms, and she has learned from this experience that action and independence are more likely to be appreciated than blind devotion and submission.

Admirers of Ibsen, the Martínez Sierras created another domestic feminist in their Spanish version of *A Doll's House, Mamá (Mama,*

1912). Ibsen's play is a feminist cornerstone in the modern theater in its defense of women's rights, for his Nora rejects both her position as doll-wife and her husband's belief that women should limit themselves to decoration, amusement, and motherhood. Nora, like many modern feminists, believes that she is simply a human being who has been victimized by the feminine tradition. She leaves home and family to search for her — and by extension woman's — true identity. Such a violent solution might have been out of character for the realistic but gentle Martínez Sierras, and it certainly would have been impractical for consumption by a middle-class Spanish audience. Mercedes, the Spanish Nora of *Mama*, fights to protect her daughter from a conniving Don Juan and learns that in active participation in affairs of the family lies her particular fulfillment. She is a feminist in denying that she is the plaything of her husband and in demanding an equal voice in making decisions. She does not leave her husband but convinces him of his mistake in seeing her as a pretty doll to be petted and pampered.

With the exception of Irene of *To Each His Own*, the heroines examined in this chapter are members of the middle or upper-middle classes. The ones who work do so because they feel compelled to express themselves and be independent. There is another group of plays made up of *La Pasión (Passion)*, *Torre de marfil (Ivory Tower)*, *La mujer del héroe (The Hero's Wife)*, *La suerte de Isabelita (Isabel's Luck)*, *El ama de casa (The Mistress of the House)*, *Madam Pepita (Mrs. Pepita)*, and some lesser titles in which the protagonists work out of economic necessity. Although these heroines are strong and admirable, they are neither liberated nor revolutionary, for they accept the menial tasks (washing, ironing, dressmaking, etc.) that tradition has assigned them and do not encroach on male territory. The liberated heroine, on the other hand, actively seeks equality with men. Energetic, ambitious, and not content to accept the traditions and conventions that ruled her mother's life, she generally feels the need to express herself outside the home. Although convinced that she has a contribution to make and unwilling to shine by glory reflected from any man, she neither forms nor joins a feminist organization but rather, singly and energetically, defends her right to be independent and equal in matters involving education and employment. These rights are related to her desire to marry for love, for she feels that education and a career free her from the marriage of convenience and make her a better wife and mother. In marriage she believes in moral equality and is happiest when she is able to be a work partner with her husband. She is an assertive, ambitious woman who very much knows what she wants from life and how to get it. The Martínez Sierra heroine was a symbol of the Spanish woman's aspirations sixty years ago; she seems on the verge of reality in our times.

While theater scholars interested in the Generation of '98 have been discovering the avant-garde qualities of Valle-Inclán, Grau and Unamuno, or rehashing the merits of Benavente, they have largely overlooked Martínez Sierra whose facile plots, homey situations, conventional dialogue, and sentimental tone have contributed to his eclipse in recent years. If one penetrates the slightly cloying surface to isolate his feminist heroine, however, one discovers an independent, equality-seeking female in sympathy with many of the goals of the current women's liberation movement. The surprise is to find such a type in so unlikely a place: Spanish commercial theater sixty years ago. This heroine may even spark a revival of interest in this somewhat forgotten but nevertheless important dramatist, particularly since we now know the latter was probably a "she" — and if not totally "she," at least androgynous.

CHAPTER 7

Conclusion

CRITICS of contemporary Spanish theater have long speculated about María Martínez Sierra's important contribution to her husband's success in the theater. Prior to the publication of this book, however, no evidence had been offered in support of María's collaboration either as writer or as consultant. Material discovered after her death in 1974 firmly establishes her as author — far more than merely inspirer or editorial assistant — of much of what was published under the name of her husband. Translations of letters and a legal document (see Chapter 2) acknowledging her collaboration are made public for the first time here.

Although the Martínez Sierras always aspired to write for the theater, they served a literary apprenticeship of approximately twelve years (1898–1910), during which time they wrote novels, stories, and articles, and translated foreign works into Spanish. Their earliest poetic essays (1898–1900), composed in the Modernist style, hindered more than helped them penetrate the commercial and bourgeois world of Spanish theater.

The early works, set rather consistently in rural Spain (particularly Asturias and León), demonstrate strong admiration for the simple, natural life. In a fashion reminiscent of Rousseau, man is portrayed as naturally good, but capable of corruption in a false environment. As long as the characters remain close to nature, they are happy; when they abandon the village, they generally become disoriented and depressed. A unifying theme of the early period is an optimistic, idealistic pantheism. The universe for Martínez Sierra is a unity with outward manifestations being expressed through phenomena. Although not a religious writer consumed with the idea of God and the goals and causes of life, Martínez Sierra is more than willing to believe that there is purpose in human existence. Although he does not mention God directly, a positive force is evident

133

in the beauty of all growing things and the elements that nurture them. Man is portrayed as naturally good but capable of corruption in an unnatural environment.

Of structural importance in these early works is the triangle pattern of two women competing for the love of one man. Frequently a Spanish woman is pitted against a foreign one, the former being consistently darkly attractive, faithful, modest, intelligent, and of impeccable virtue, while the latter — large, ungainly, and irritatingly superficial, — is of easy virtue. This exaltation of the native product, frequently reinforced through a mild xenophobia, runs contrary to the period's general rejection by Spanish intellectuals of things Spanish. Partly because traditional authors of the nineteenth century enshrined Spanishness, the writers of the Generation of '98 reacted against this attitude of their elders and sought solutions outside traditional and local molds.

Once the Martínez Sierras recognized that their true interest was in people rather than the landscape, they no longer personified nature. Their characters after about 1905 become flesh-and-blood people (as in *You Are Peace* and *Ivory Tower*) rather than symbols through whom to express ideas (as in *Labor's Poem, Fantastic Dialogues, Frost Flowers, The Mute Jungle, The Hopeful Pilgrim*, and others). The very human character types that emerge toward the end of the apprenticeship period persist strongly in the theater: the strong but feminine woman, the tyrannical mother, and the weak-willed man. While they abandon the exaggeratedly favorable comparison of a graceful, charming, modest Spanish woman to a clumsy, immoral foreign one, they continue to demonstrate much admiration for the traditional Spanish virtues, especially as exemplified in women. After 1910, they will draw their characters almost exclusively from recognizable members of Spanish society.

In addition to shifts in style, setting, and character, the Martínez Sierras adopt an increasingly optimistic, even playful, attitude toward life (i.e., *Blessed Spring* and *All Is One and the Same*). After *Cradle Song* (1911), they do not return to the pessimism of *Frost Flowers*, nor will they close their works abruptly amidst fear, moans of frustration, or cries of terror as they frequently did in the early works. While the admirable women of the early novels and stories are portrayed as consolers, content only when submerging their frustrations in the problems of others, the female characters of the plays gradually become positive about overcoming their limitations and emerge as the most successful ingredient of Martínez Sierra's literary creations. After some experimentation, the authors found their characters, style, and message in *Mistress of the House* (1910).

Despite the sentimental and bourgeois tenor of *Mistress of the House* and the many plays that followed it, Martínez Sierra sought to elevate theater tastes through the ambitious program of foreign and Spanish drama he provided at the Eslava Theater during his eight years there as artistic director. Notwithstanding his conventional public image, Martínez Sierra was a liberal artist and an intellectual who favored reforming outmoded social systems, especially as they applied to women and the disadvantaged. His revolt, gently couched, found expression in the feminist plays as well as in those plays featuring maternal nuns. At the heart of the latter plays is a plea for heartfelt rather than dutiful charity in the interest of a better life for all.

Although not an iconoclast, Martínez Sierra seems not to favor the cloistered life. The nuns of *Cradle Song, Lily Among Thorns,* and *The Kingdom of God* are happiest when working to find an outlet for their social and maternal impulses. Not mysterious, ethereal, or even particularly spiritual, these nuns enjoy participating actively in the world of people rather than of ideas or abstractions. Consistently moderate in their approach to almost everything, the Martínez Sierras favor a balance of physical, emotional, and spiritual expression, blending in their writings idealism with realism. Their practical goal is the healthy mind in the healthy body through simple health rules, work, love, and charity. Although some have criticized Martínez Sierra for a childlike naiveté and lack of masculine vigor, others strongly defend his optimism, his healthy enthusiasm for life and defend his style as totally human in that it combines both masculine and feminine qualities.

Despite their insistence that women are essentially mothers and that maternity is the loftiest expression of femininity, the Martínez Sierras are apologists for women's rights. Their feminism is personal and relates almost exclusively to the special situation of the woman in Spanish society. It is, moreover, essentially a sexist feminism in that women are portrayed as superior in morality, intellect, and *voluntad* (will). The feminist heroines are diplomatically aggressive in pushing for equality of rights and responsibilities. Although frequently professional women, they first seek equality in the marriage relationship. As wives, they insist that their husbands adhere to the same moral standards set for women and feel that they have as much right to express themselves professionally — and as much duty to support the marriage economically — as men.

Despite María's active involvement in the Spanish feminist movement, the word feminism is never mentioned in the plays, and no character is ever involved in an organization for women's rights. The Martínez Sierras do, however, advocate careers for women, particularly in education, medicine, literature, and the social services. They portray women as happier when performing work outside the domestic chores, although these too are important and have dignity. The ideal arrangement, the Martínez Sierras suggest, is the professional collaboration of husband and wife, for then both marriage and career enjoy maximum support. This ideal of professional and personal collaboration was one that Gregorio and María lived for many years and partially accounts for the frequency with which they portrayed it.

Although the Martínez Sierras wrote prolifically in the areas of novel, short story, essay, and poetry, it is as dramatists that they will best be remembered. Their major single contribution in this area is *Cradle Song*, still a standard inclusion in modern international theater repertory. The name of Martínez Sierra also remains before the public as author of the librettos of the frequently performed ballets, *El sombrero de tres picos (The Three-Cornered Hat)* and *El amor brujo (Love's Sorcery)*. Moreover, María's personal legacy to Spanish women endures in the various educational and cultural organizations she initiated in the 1930's. Similarly, the reading public continues to reap the benefits of Gregorio's literary concerns through the publication of many works by major as well as minor literary figures of his day. In addition, his innovative spirit in the area of theatrical direction has provided inspiration as well as a practical model for other Spanish directors, among whom he continues to be highly respected. Perhaps the realization that the Martínez Sierras continue, even though quietly, to exert force on artistic and cultural life both inside and outside of Spain will spark a revival of interest in this unusual couple, eclipsed in recent years by more flamboyant members of their generation.

Notes and References

All undated articles and unpublished papers quoted in this book are on file in a special collection of Gregorio and María Martínez Sierra documents in the University of Cincinnati Library.

Chapter One

1. For more information on Modernism and the Generation of '98, see: Pedro Laín Entralgo, *La generación del '98* (Madrid: 1948) and Guillermo Díaz Plaja, *Modernismo frente a noventa y ocho* (Madrid: Espasa-Calpe, 1966).

2. Andrés Goldsborough Serrat, *Imagen humana y literaria de Gregorio Martínez Sierra* (Madrid, 1965), p. 11.

3. María Martínez Sierra, *Gregorio y yo* (Mexico, 1953), pp. 23–24.

4. Andrés Goldsborough Serrat, p. 13.

5. *Ibid.*, p. 14.

6. *Ibid.*, p. 16.

7. María Martínez Sierra, *Una mujer por los caminos de España* (Buenos Aires, 1953), p. 181.

8. Friends of Gregorio agree that his religion (as well as his politics) was to live the good life and to succeed. Gregorio did, however, receive the final sacraments of the Roman Catholic Church before his death.

9. *Gregorio y yo*, p. 25.

10. *Ibid.*, p. 27.

11. *Ibid.*, p. 28.

12. *Ibid.*, p. 45.

13. *Una mujer por los caminos de España*, p. 33.

14. Ricardo Gullón, in *Relaciones amistosas y literarias entre Juan Ramón Jiménez y los Martínez Sierra* (Río Piedras, 1961), p. 40, calls *Helios* the most important Modernist journal. *Helios* also published works by Azorín, much of Ganivet's *Epistolario*, and works by Antonio and Manuel Machado.

15. With the passage of time, María forgot the authors of the works winning first and second place, remembering only that the first prize went

to a novel called *Cuartel de inválidos*. See María's prologue to *Tú eres la paz* (Madrid:Espasa-Calpe, 1965), p. 7.

16. *Gregorio y yo*, p. 41.

17. *Ibid.*, p. 177.

18. Ricardo Gullón states (p. 40): "I understand that *You Are Peace* continues to be read, and when I have asked my students (especially in America) if they have read any work by the Martínez Sierras and which one, I learn that this is the fiction most often known by some of them."

19. *Gregorio y yo*, pp. 60–61.

20. This is an evaluation given by Catalina's daughter.

21. *Gregorio y yo*, p. 258.

22. *Ibid.*, p. 27.

23. See: *Gregorio y yo*, p. 26; *Una mujer por los caminos de España*, p. 182; "María Lejárraga de Martínez Sierra: la vida comienza a los ochenta," n.d., n.p., n. pag.

24. A more interesting and plausible explanation of this penchant for tearing up dolls is offered in *El amor catedrático* (*Love Is the Teacher*, 1910), a novel featuring a young girl who could well have been María's alter ego. (The literary alter ego was common practice among writers of the period.) The central character explains that only a great love can inspire violence and that destruction is a form of possession: "It took me long, tedious months of heartless and latent love to discover that only the man we love with all our heart is capable of inspiring in us the imperious desire to scratch, which at times startles us; to scratch, to bite, to tear up. No doubt it is that anxiety of possession manifested in the instinct to exercise one of the rights of possessor: to destroy the possessed article — something like that zeal children take in tearing up their toys which researchers have discovered to be a basic manifestation of the constructive instinct" (Buenos Aires: Espasa-Calpe, 1925, p. 24). Although María publicly interpreted her delight in destroying dolls as a lack of maternal instinct, she demonstrates familiarity with the contrary theory. Destruction, she suggests, can be symbolic of the desire to possess, create, and construct, a concept related to — and clearly in harmony with — the maternal instinct.

25. *Gregorio y yo*, p. 270.

26. *Ibid.*, p. 65.

27. *Ibid.*, p. 68.

28. *Ibid.*, p. 277.

29. *Ibid.*, p. 278.

30. *Un teatro de arte* (Madrid: Ediciones de la Esfinge, 1926), p. 9.

31. See the feminist essays: *Cartas a las mujeres de España* (1916), *Feminismo, feminidad, españolismo* (1917), *La mujer moderna* (1920).

32. This critic, who wishes his name withheld, considers himself a friend of Gregorio and Catalina. He apparently relates feminism to radical politics and sexual license.

33. "La vida comienza a los ochenta: María Lejárraga de Martínez Sierra," n.d., n.p., n.pag.

34. Gregorio had, in effect, ceased to hold the economic whip. It is perhaps significant that no new play was published after the 1930 agreement.

35. All information about Gregorio in Hollywood is contained in letters from him.

36. *Una mujer por los caminos de España*, p. 108.

37. *Ibid.*, p. 69.

38. Catalina Bárcena, the only surviving member of a fascinating triangle, is now completely deaf and suffers from various health problems only partially alleviated by long vacations in the Canary Islands.

39. *Gregorio y yo*, p. 13.

40. An article by Ramón Antonio Chas, "¿Por qué no firmó María Martínez Sierra las obras que escribió con su esposo?" n.d., n.p., n.pag.

41. "Los cien años felices de María Martínez Sierra," *Los domingos de A B C* (March 3, 1974), p. 25.

Chapter Two

1. Years before, Gregorio had chosen to live in an insane asylum in order to study the mentally ill before undertaking the writing of the novel *Almas ausentes* (1900).

2. Of course, I neither spoke to every member of the company nor to all of María's family. Those contacted gave me this impression.

3. Of their peaceful relationship, María writes: "In all our years of intimacy, I do not recall a single harsh word: He was one of those rare persons with perfect self-control" (*Gregorio y yo*, p. 278). Another possibility is that María never provoked him.

4. Catalina, some say, represented herself as Gregorio's wife outside of Spain. Although information in the *A B C* (Spanish newspaper) file lists her as married to Martínez Sierra, no legal ceremony was ever performed. Neither María nor Gregorio ever sought a legal separation.

5. Photocopies on file at the University of Cincinnati library.

6. An irony of the model Martínez Sierra woman is that Catalina, who hardly resembled her personally, incarnated her on stage to perfection. Whether Gregorio fell in love with the fictional character, the professional Catalina, or the real Catalina is another question.

7. Introduction to *The Plays of Sierra*, translated by John Garrett Underhill (London, 1923), 1, ix.

8. *The McGraw-Hill Encyclopedia of Works of Drama* (New York: The McGraw-Hill Book Co., 1972), 3, 112.

9. Gonzalo Torrente Ballester, *Panorama de la literatura española contemporánea* (Madrid, 1956), pp. 339–40.

10. *A New History of Spanish Literature* (Baton Rouge: Louisiana State University Press, 1961), p. 154.

11. *Literatura española contemporánea* (Salamanca: Ediciones Anaya, 1965), p. 168.

12. *Historia de la literatura española: Siglo veinte* (Barcelona: Ariel, 1974), p. 182.

13. *Brief Survey of Spanish Literature* (Patterson, N.J.: Littlefield, Adams & Co., 1960), p. 154.

14. *Artículos de crítica teatral: El teatro español de 1914 a 1936* (Mexico, 1968), I, 28.

15. *Historia del teatro español: Siglo veinte* (Madrid, 1971), p. 57.

16. *Historia de la lengua y literatura castellanas* (Madrid, 1919), XII, 177. Subsequent references will appear in the text.

17. *El teatro español hoy* (Barcelona, 1975), p. 24.

18. *Contemporary Spanish Literature* (New York, 1925), p. 176. Incidentally, *La mujer del héroe* and *Pobrecito Juan* do not represent feminist views.

19. Gullón. Quotations are taken from pages 9, 10, 14, and 20.

20. Pedro González Blanco, "Notas," n.d., n.p., n.pag.

21. *Teatro* (Madrid: Aguilar, 1948), p. 18.

22. *Novela* (Madrid: Aguilar, 1962), p. 22.

23. Goldsborough Serrat, p. 17. It would not surprise me to learn that this book had been commissioned by Catalina Bárcena.

24. Peón de Brega, "Presencias," n.d., n.p., n.pag.

25. Arturo de Romay, "Cumplirá 90 años la juventud de María Martínez Sierra," n.d., n.p., n.pag.

26. Indalecio Prieto, "Una mujer excepcional: María Lejárraga de Martínez Sierra," n.d., n.p., n.pag.

27. W. K. Mayo, "Canción de cuna" in *El comercio*, n.d., n.pag.

28. From the "Foro" ("Forum") of *Excelsiór*, n.d., n.pag. The headline reads: "Es cierto lo de doña María Lejárraga de Martínez Sierra" ("What They Say About María Lejárraga de Martínez Sierra Is True").

29. This note, included in María's personal papers, has not been published previously.

30. Arthur L. Owen, ed., *El ama de la casa* (Chicago: B. H. Sanborn and Co., 1928), p. xv.

31. *Gregorio y yo*, p. 47.

32. *Ibid.*, pp. 29–30.

33. *Ibid.*

34. Ramón Antonio Chas, "¿Por qué no firmó María Martínez Sierra las obras que escribió con su esposo?", n.d., n.p., n.pag.

35. "Evoca los recuerdos de su vida en Europa y América la señora María Martínez Sierra," n.d., n.p., n.pag.

36. *Ibid.*

37. Ramón Antonio Chas, "¿Por qué no firmó María Martínez Sierra las obras que escribió con su esposo?", n.d., n.p., n.pag.

38. "Evoca los recuerdos de su vida en Europa y América la señora María Martínez Sierra," n.d., n.p., n.pag.

39. *Ibid.*

40. All correspondence quoted here is on file in the University of Cincinnati Library.

41. Josefina Carabias, "A los cien años, escribiendo . . ." *Ya* (Madrid) Aug. 8, 1974, p. 8.

42. José Prat, "Nota de teatro: María Martínez Sierra," *El Tiempo* (Bogota), July 30, 1974, p. 28.

43. Ángel Lázaro, "Una española eminente," *La Vanguardia* (Barcelona) Aug. 5, 1974, p. 16.

44. From an article entitled: "La vida comienza a los ochenta," n.d., n.p., n.pag.

45. *Ibid.*

46. *Ibid.*

47. *Gregorio y yo*, p. 11.

48. *Ibid.*

49. Outside of titles published in the "Colección Austral" (*Tú eres la paz, Canción de cuna* and *El amor catedrático*), works by Gregorio Martínez Sierra are difficult if not impossible to obtain in Spain. Several school editions published in this country remain available: *Canción de cuna* (Heath), *Sueño de nua noche de agosto* (Holt and Norton) and *Mamá* (Norton).

50. One of them is published in this book. I particularly like this picture — the only one I saw of both Gregorio and María — because it tells a story: it shows María hard at work writing while Gregorio simply contemplates her activity. (Perhaps he is thinking of ideas to suggest to her?) This picture, reflecting the division of labor, came to me more and more frequently as I did the research on this book.

51. Both Ucelay and La Gorbea were dramatists.

52. Photocopy on file in the University of Cincinnati Library.

Chapter Three

1. Gullón, p. 12.

2. *Ibid.*

3. See the chapter on "The Weak Man Contrasted to the Strong Woman" in Patricia W. O'Connor, *Women in the Theater of Gregorio Martínez Sierra* (New York, 1967).

4. *Gregorio y yo*, p. 45.

5. *Obras completas* (Madrid: Renacimiento, 1921), XXIV, 12.

6. *Gregorio y yo*, p. 45.

7. *Obras completas*, XXIV, 15.

8. *Ibid.*, p. 19.
9. *Ibid.*, p. 81.
10. *Ibid.*, pp. 82–83.
11. *El agua dormida* (Madrid, 1909), p. 16.
12. *Gregorio y yo*, p. 46.
13. *Ibid.*, p. 33.
14. From an article published in Buenos Aires approximately in 1965 entitled: "Evoca los recuerdos de su vida en Europa y América la señora María Martínez Sierra," n.d., n.p., n.pag.
15. *Ibid.*
16. *Obras completas*, XXIV, 109.
17. *Gregorio y yo*, p. 34.
18. *Obras completas*, XXIV, 204.
19. *Almas ausentes* (Madrid: Renacimiento, 1921), p. 163.
20. *Gregorio y yo*, p. 32.
21. *Tú eres la paz* and *Horas de sol* (Madrid: Espasa-Calpe, 1965), p. 425.
22. *Ibid.*, p. 445.
23. *Ibid.*
24. *El agua dormida*, pp. 17–18.
25. *Pascua florida* (Barcelona: Editorial Salvat, 1919), p. 28.
26. *Ibid.*, p. 39.
27. *Cartas a las mujeres de España* (1916), *Feminismo, feminidad, españolismo* (1917), *La mujer moderna* (1920), *Nuevas cartas a las mujeres* (1932), *Cartas a las mujeres de América* (1941).
28. *Pascua florida*, p. 78.
29. *Ibid.*, p. 34.
30. Martínez Sierra's admiration for work may be related to his worship of the sun and heat in general. Both work and exposure to the sun produce warmth.
31. *Los contemporáneos* (Paris, 1907), Series I, II, 52–53.
32. See the chapter on "The Mother: A Symbol of Conservatism" in Patricia W. O'Connor, *Women in the Theater of Gregorio Martínez Sierra* (New York, 1967).
33. *Sol de la tarde* (Madrid: Renacimiento, 1921), p. 77.
34. González Blanco, p. 59.
35. *Sol de la tarde*, p. 218.
36. Aurelio Espinosa, ed., *Teatro de ensueño* (New York: World Book Co., 1920), p. 9.
37. *Ibid.*, p. 17.
38. *Ibid.*, p. 27.
39. *Ibid.*
40. *Ibid.*, p. 32.
41. *Gregorio y yo*, p. 34.
42. *La humilde verdad* (Madrid: Renacimiento, 1917), p. 195.

43. *Gregorio y yo*, p. 290.

44. *Abril melancólico* (Madrid, 1916), p. 300.

45. *El agua dormida* (Madrid, 1909), p. 75.

46. *Abril melancólico*, p. 203.

47. *Ibid.*, pp. 204–205.

48. The characters and situation remind one of Ramón Pérez de Ayala's novel *Luna de miel, luna de hiel*. Micaela, Cástulo, and Urbano are similar to the marchioness, the preceptor, and Gabriel.

49. *Abril melancólico*, p. 228.

50. *Ibid.*, p. 235.

51. *Ibid.*, p. 257.

52. In character and action, Gabriel also bears much similarity to Ariel of Casona's *La casa de los siete balcones*.

53. *Abril melancólico*, p. 200.

54. *El peregrino ilusionado* (Madrid: Renacimiento, 1921), p. 10.

55. *Ibid.*, p. 93.

56. *La selva muda* (Madrid: Renacimiento, 1921), p. 8.

57. *El amor catedrático* (Buenos Aires: Espasa-Calpe, 1955), p. 162.

58. *Ibid.*, p. 158.

59. *Ibid.*, p. 130.

60. *Ibid.*, p. 167.

61. *Ibid.*

62. *Ibid.*

63. Julio Cejador y Frauca, in *Historia de la lengua y literatura castellanas* (Madrid, 1919) writes: "In his impressionistic interest in landscape and detail, he resembles Azorín, although he handles language much better and is more poetic, while Azorín is prosaic. What is free-flowing and unencumbered in Martínez Sierra is uneven and heavy in Azorín" XII, 143.

Chapter Four

1. In *Gregorio y yo* (pp. 40–41), María Martínez Sierra mentions an early version of *Mama* presented to a literary contest in 1904. Because this version is not available, I will not consider *Mama*, successfully performed in 1913, here.

2. *Gregorio y yo*, p. 43.

3. Indeed María labels him an "antifeminist who never understood women" (*Ibid.*, pp. 51–52).

4. *Teatro* (Madrid: Aguilar, 1948), p. 89. Future references to this work will appear in the text.

5. One theme of this play, however, concerns the necessary influence of both parents.

6. The appreciation of his wife as a "sex object" reinforces the *machista* tone of the play. I make this point only because Martínez Sierra later

became such a staunch feminist and defender of the Spanish woman in many plays.

7. Not entirely accurately, Walter Starkie states in "Gregorio Martínez Sierra and the Modern Spanish Drama," *Contemporary Review*, 125 (Feb. 1924), 202: "In vain we look through his plays for one strong personality of the male sex." In addition to Don José of *La sombra del padre*, other strong male characters appear in *Esperanza nuestra* (1917), *Los pastores* (1913), and *Seamos felices* (1929).

8. *El ama de la casa*, ed. Arthur L. Owen (Chicago: B. H. Sanborn and Co., 1926), p. 24. Future references to this work will appear in the text.

Chapter Five

1. Cansinos Assens, however, observed in *Poetas y prosistas* (p. 276) that: "With *Holy Night* and *The Kingdom of God*, Martínez Sierra seemed to initiate a new trend toward a cordial Christian democracy. . . ," and Camilo María Abad in his article "La obra de Martínez Sierra: el teatro" states: "*Cradle Song* . . . *Lily Among Thorns*, and *The Kingdom of God* could also be included in what one might call social plays" (*Razón y Fe*, 64 [1925], 150).

2. This novice recalls Pérez de Ayala's virgin, Simona, of *Luna de miel, luna de hiel*. In her innocence, Simona believed she was pregnant and carrying the child in her throat. The displacement of the sexual passageway is interesting and a perfectly valid manifestation of repression.

3. In the course of the poetic interlude of the play, Martínez Sierra demonstrates his belief that women desire sexual contact only to have children. While Freud would probably stress early childhood frustrations and the lack of sexual outlet in the pathology of these nuns, Martínez Sierra, considering sexual union merely a procedural necessity of maternity, would insist that sexual frustration was only a component of the maternal drive.

4. "Gregorio Martínez Sierra and the Modern Spanish Drama," *Contemporary Review*, 125 (Feb. 1924), 200.

5. There is nothing else mystical about this play, however.

6. Underhill, I, 22. Future references to this edition will appear in the text.

7. María Martínez Sierra considered her, rather than Sister Juana, the central character of *Cradle Song*. See: *Gregorio y yo*, pp. 275–76.

8. In its emphasis on women as exclusively and essentially mothers, *Cradle Song* belies but does not contradict the feminist attitude that would soon emerge (approximately 1915). In this play, women are simple creatures, as elemental as salmon, single-mindedly and instinctually battling the current to spawn.

9. *Lirio entre espinas* (Madrid: Prensa Moderna, 1927), p. 9. Future references to this edition will appear in the text.

10. It is interesting to note the use of the name Teresa. Although in *Cradle Song* Teresa was the "child of sin" and perhaps even the child of an inhabitant of a brothel, she came to save her virginal mothers. Although Teresa had no vocation for the convent in *Cradle Song*, we find a Sister Teresa in this subsequent work. Here she may have come full circle in that she returns to her origins, perhaps even to her mother, whom she will, ironically, mother.

11. When Sister Teresa asks to spend the night, the men respond to the request as though she were a new member of the house. This talking at cross-purposes continues until the prostitutes intervene to defend the nun.

12. Sister Gracia fits the description that the Martínez Sierras make of Celia in Galdós' *Celia en los infiernos (Celia in the Underworld)*, suggesting thereby that their character may have been inspired by this Galdós heroine. In writing of the earlier play, the Martínez Sierras express great admiration for Celia, the child of a wealthy family whose conscience will not permit her to live in ease while others exist in misery. Celia, like Sister Gracia, descends to the "underworld" of poverty where man's only sin is to have been born poor. Of the inhabitants in this hell, the Martínez Sierras continue: "They are exploited by the insatiable greed of industry, by the heartless voracity of capital without a conscience" (*Feminismo, feminidad, españolismo*, p. 189).

13. Underhill, II, 27. Future references to this edition will appear in the text.

14. Although they do not feature nuns, other plays similarly socialistic in theme are *El palacio triste (The Sad Palace*, 1911) and *Esperanza nuestra (The Hope That Is Ours*, 1917).

15. Although Martínez Sierra never openly quarreled with Church dogma or politics, there is strong implicit condemnation of certain customs and practices that interfere with the natural expression of human fraternity.

16. Philip Hereford, trans., *Holy Night* (New York: E. P. Dutton and Co., Inc., 1928), p. 48. Future references to this edition will appear in the text.

17. A priest of *The Shepherds* also illustrates the renunciation theme. In his selfless dedication to his parishoners, he illustrates the ideal of human (not merely feminine) generosity that Martínez Sierra frequently portrays in women through the metaphor of the maternal instinct.

18. Obviously, I do not agree with Walter Starkie, who in an article that includes reference to *The Kingdom of God*, writes: "Perhaps the greatest virtue of Martínez Sierra is that he abolished that ideal of renunciation in drama which had lasted into the twentieth century and which cast its pall over literature. His heroines do not, as many of the Benaventian heroines do, sacrifice themselves in order that others may be happy" ("Gregorio Martínez Sierra and the Modern Spanish Drama," *Contemporary Review*, 125 [Feb. 1924], 205).

Chapter Six

1. *Feminismo, feminidad, españolismo* (Madrid: Renacimiento: 1920), pp. 17–18.
2. Walter Starkie, in a study of Martínez Sierra's plays ("Gregorio Martínez Sierra and Modern Spanish Drama," *Contemporary Review*, 125 [February, 1924], 198–205), recalls no strong man. I suggest that he does exist but concede that he is no match for the heroine.
3. *Obras completas*, XIII, 85.
4. *Ibid.*, p. 90.
5. *Ibid.*, p. 91.
6. *Cada uno y su vida*, (Madrid: Estrella, 1924), pp. 139–40.
7. See Patricia W. O'Connor, "La madre española en el teatro de Gregorio Martínez Sierra," *Duquesne Hispanic Review*, IV, 1 (Spring 1965), 17–24.
8. As in *Canción de cuna, Lirio entre espinas, El reino de Dios, Navidad, El palacio triste, Mamá, Primavera en otoño, La mujer del héroe, El ama de la casa,* and to a lesser extent in other plays.
9. *Obras completas*, X, 117.
10. *Ibid.*, 112.
11. *Ibid.*, IV, 99.
12. *Sueño de una noche de agosto*, ed. May Gardner and Arthur L. Owen (New York: Holt, Rinehart and Winston, 1967), pp. 13–14.
13. *Ibid.*, pp. 32–33.
14. *Ibid.*, p. 33.
15. *Ibid.*, p. 38.
16. *Ibid.*, pp. 14–15.

Selected Bibliography

PRIMARY SOURCES

(signed by Gregorio Martínez Sierra)

El poema del trabajo. Madrid: Eusebio Sánchez, 1898.
Diálogos fantásticos. Madrid: A. Pérez y P. García, 1899.
Flores de escarcha. Madrid: G. Sastre, 1900.
Almas ausentes. Madrid: Biblioteca Mignón, 1900.
Horas de sol. Madrid: Ambrosio Pérez y Cía., 1901.
Pascua florida. Barcelona: Salvat y Cía., 1903.
Sol de la tarde. Madrid: Tipografía de la Revista de Archivos, 1904.
La humilde verdad. Madrid: Henrich y Cía., 1905.
La tristeza del Quixote. Madrid: Biblioteca Nacional, 1905.
Teatro de ensueño. Madrid: Imprenta de Samarám y Cía., 1905.
Motivos. Paris: Garnier, 1905.
Tú eres la paz. Madrid: Montaner y Simón, 1906.
La feria de Neuilly. Paris: Garnier, 1906.
Aldea ilusoria. Paris: Garnier, 1907.
La casa de la primavera. Madrid: Renacimiento, 1907.
Aventura. Madrid: Blas y Cía., 1907.
Aventura and *Beata primavera.* Madrid: Renacimiento, 1908.
El peregrino ilusionado. Paris: Garnier, 1908.
Torre de marfil. Madrid: El Cuento Semanal, 1908.
Juventud, divino tesoro. Madrid: Renacimiento, 1908.
Hechizo de amor. Madrid: V. Prieto, 1908.
La selva muda. Madrid: Blass y Cía., 1909.
El agua dormida. Madrid: Sucesores de Hernando, 1909.
La sombra del padre. Madrid: Tipografía de la Revista de Archivos, 1909.
El ama de la casa. Madrid: Sucesores de Hernando, 1910.
El amor catedrático. Barcelona: E. Domenech, 1910.
Todo es uno y lo mismo. Madrid: Revista de Archivos, 1910.
Primavera en otoño. Madrid: Prieto y Cía., 1911.

147

Canción de cuna. Madrid: R. Velasco, 1911.
El palacio triste. Madrid: Renacimiento, 1911.
La suerte de Isabelita. Madrid: Velasco, 1911.
Lirio entre espinas. Madrid: Velasco, 1911.
El pobrecito Juan. Madrid: Editorial Prieto y Cía., 1912.
Madam Pepita. Madrid: Renacimiento, 1912.
El enamorado. Madrid: Renacimiento, 1913.
Mamá. Madrid: Renacimiento, 1913.
Sólo par mujeres. Madrid: R. Velasco, 1913.
Madrigal. Madrid: Renacimiento, 1913.
Los pastores. Madrid: R. Velasco, 1913.
La vida inquieta. Madrid: Renacimiento, 1913.
La tirana. Madrid: Renacimiento, 1913.
Margot. Madrid: Renacimiento, 1914.
Las golondrinas. Madrid: Juan Pueyo, 1914.
La mujer del héroe. Madrid: R. Velasco, 1914.
La pasión. Madrid: Renacimiento, 1914.
El amor brujo. Madrid: Velasco, 1915.
Amanecer. Madrid: R. Velasco, 1915.
El reino de Dios. Madrid: Pueyo, 1916.
El diablo se ríe. Madrid: Renacimiento, 1916.
Abril melancólico. Madrid: Renacimiento, 1916.
Cartas a las mujeres de España. Madrid: Clásica Española, 1916.
Esperanza nuestra. Madrid: Renacimiento, 1917.
Navidad. Madrid: Renacimiento, 1916.
Feminismo, feminidad, españolismo. Madrid: Renacimiento, 1917.
La adúltera penitente. Madrid: Renacimiento, 1917.
Calendario espiritual. Madrid: Estrella, 1918.
Cristo niño. Madrid: Estrella, 1918.
Sueño de una noche de agosto. Madrid: Renacimiento, 1918.
Rosina es frágil. Madrid: Estrella, 1918.
Cada uno y su vida. Madrid: Estrella, 1919.
El corazón ciego. Madrid: Estrella, 1919.
Fuente serena. Madrid: Estrella, 1919.
La mujer moderna. Madrid: Estrella, 1920.
Vida y dulzura. Madrid: Renacimiento, 1920.
Granada. Madrid: Estrella, 1920.
Kodak Romántico. Madrid: Estrella, 1921.
El ideal. Madrid: Estrella, 1921.
Don Juan de España. Madrid: Estrella, 1921.
Torre de marfil. Madrid: Estrella, 1924.
Cada uno y su vida. Madrid: Prensa Gráfica, 1924.
Mujer. Madrid: Estrella, 1925.
Rosas mustias. Madrid: Prensa Gráfica, 1926.

Seamos felices. Madrid: Estrella, 1929.
Triángulo. Madrid: Estrella, 1930.
La hora del diablo. Madrid: Estrella, 1930.
Eva curiosa. Madrid: Pence, 1930.
Nuevas cartas a las mujeres. Madrid: Ibero Americana de Publicaciones, 1932.
Cartas a las mujeres de América. Buenos Aires: Renacimiento, 1941.

(signed by María Martínez Sierra)

She is also the author of a number of stories and articles published in Buenos Aires, principally in *La Prensa,* after 1953.
Cuentos breves. Madrid: Imprenta de Enrique Rojas, 1899.
La mujer española ante la república. Madrid: Ediciones de Esfinge, 1931.
Una mujer por los caminos de España. Buenos Aires: Losada, 1952.
Gregorio y yo. Mexico: Biografías Gandesa, 1953.
Viajes de una gota de agua. Buenos Aires: Librería Hachette S.A., 1954.
Fiesta en el Olimpo. Buenos Aires: Aguilar, 1960.

SECONDARY SOURCES

1. Books

BASTINOS, ANTONIO. *Arte dramático español contemporáneo.* Barcelona: Imprenta Elzeviriana, 1914, pp. 81–82. Short essays on over one hundred dramatists of the nineteenth and twentieth centuries. Martínez Sierra called one of the most successful of contemporary Spanish dramatists; his gentle optimism lauded.

BELL, AUBREY F. *Contemporary Spanish Literature.* New York: Alfred A. Knopf, 1925, pp. 171–78. Emphasizes Martínez Sierra's theatrical characters.

CANSINOS ASSENS, RAFAEL. *La nueva literatura.* Madrid: Editorial Paez, 1925, 1, 171–83. Flowery praise of Martínez Sierra's early period.

———. *Poetas y prosistas.* Madrid: Editorial Americana, 1919, pp. 276–89. Among other things, this author deals with literary influences on Gregorio Martínez Sierra.

CEJADOR Y FRAUCA, JULIO. *Historia de la lengua y literatura castellanas.* Madrid: Tipografía de la Revista de Archivos, 1919, 12, 177–95. Cejador particularly admires the totally human quality of Martínez Sierra's work and attributes this balance to the joint authorship of a man and a woman.

DIAZ-PLAJA, GUILLERMO. *Modernismo frente a noventa y ocho.* Madrid: Espasa-Calpe, 1966. Separates Modernism from the Generation of '98.

DIEZ-CANEDO, ENRIQUE. *Artículos de crítica teatral: El teatro español de 1914 a 1936.* Mexico: Joaquín Mortiz, S.A., 1968, 1, 293–302. Reviews performances of *Mujer, Torre de marfil, La hija de todos, Cada uno y su vida, Seamos felices,* and *Triángulo.*

GARCÍA LORENZO, LUCIANO. *El teatro español hoy.* Barcelona: Editorial Planeta, 1975, pp. 24–28. This critic prefers the stage director to the writer.

GOLDSBOROUGH SERRAT, ANDRÉS. *Imagen humana y literaria de Gregorio Martínez Sierra.* Madrid: Gráficos Cóndor, 1965. Totally ignores the existence — to say nothing of the influence — of María in the life and works of Gregorio Martínez Sierra.

GONZÁLEZ BLANCO, ANDRÉS. *Los contemporáneos.* Paris: Garnier, 1906, series 1, 2, 1–74. Enthusiastic praise of Martínez Sierra's ability to write about nature in delicate rather than bold terms.

GRANJEL, LUIS S. *La generación literaria del noventa y ocho.* Salamanca: Anaya, 1966. Classifies Martínez Sierra with the Modernists.

GUERRERO ZAMORA, JUAN. *Historia del teatro contemporáneo, II.* Barcelona: Juan Flors, 1971. Ignores Martínez Sierra, the dramatist, to concentrate on the generous and innovative director.

GULLÓN, RICARDO. *Relaciones amistosas y literarias entre Juan Ramón Jiménez y los Martínez Sierra.* Río Piedras: Ediciones de la Torre, 1961. Publishes significant correspondence between Juan Ramón Jimenez and María and Gregorio Martínez Sierra preceded by an important biographical introduction.

MARTÍNEZ SIERRA, GREGORIO, ed. *Un teatro de arte en España.* Madrid: Ediciones la Esfinge, 1926. Essays by Manuel Abril, Tomás Borrás, Cansinos Assens, Eduardo Marquina, and others in praise of Martínez Sierra's theatrical innovations in the Eslava Theater.

O'CONNOR, PATRICIA W. *Women in the Theater of Gregorio Martínez Sierra.* New York: American Press, 1967. Study of the feminist heroine, the idealized mother, the negative mother, the ingenue and the kindly grandmother. A final chapter treats the generally weak man.

PÉREZ DE AYALA, RAMÓN. *Las máscaras,* 2. Madrid: Clásica española, 1917. Critiques of Martínez Sierra's versions (translation as well as direction) of Shakespeare's *Taming of the Shrew* and Ibsen's *A Doll's House.*

RUIZ RAMÓN, FRANCISCO. *Historia del teatro español, 2: Siglo Veinte.* Madrid: Alianza Editorial, 1971, 54–59. Classifies Martínez Sierra as the "soft" wing (as opposed to the "harsh" one represented by Linares Rivas) of the Benaventine school and deals primarily with the feminine component of the plays.

SAINZ DE ROBLES, FEDERICO CARLOS. *Deccionario de la literatura.* Madrid: Aguilar, 1959, pp. 679–80. Rather indiscriminate praise of Martínez Sierra as poet, novelist, dramatist, editor, publisher, and theater director.

———. "Nota preliminar" to *Teatro* (*La sombra del padre* and *Don Juan de España,* #233; *Novela* (*Tú eres la paz* and *Horas de sol*) #234; *Ensayos*

(*Granada* and *Cartas a las mujeres de España*), #235. Madrid: Aguilar (Colección Crisol), 1948. Praises Martínez Sierra rather indiscriminately and finds his poetry and novels superior to his plays. Some biographical information also.

TORRENTE BALLESTER, GONZALO. *Panorama de la literatura española contemporánea.* Madrid: Ediciones Guadarrama, 1956, pp. 339–40. Criticizes the lack of "virility" in the works and prefers the lighter plays to the more serious ones.

——. *Teatro español contemporáneo.* Madrid: Ediciones Guadarrama, 1968, pp. 304–06. Negative criticism of *Don Juan de España.*

TURRELL, CHARLES ALFRED. *Contemporary Spanish Dramatists.* Boston: The Gorham Press, 1919, pp. 19–20. In addition to the publication in English of plays by Galdós, Linares Rivas, Álvarez Quintero, Zamacois and Dicenta, an introductory chapter about contemporary Spanish theater classifies Martínez Sierra as ultranational, lyrical, and feminine in his works.

VALBUENA PRAT, ANGEL. *Historia de la literatura española.* Barcelona: Gustavo Gil, S.A., 1946, 2, 815–18. Finds Martínez Sierra's work excessively sentimental and uncomplicated.

——. *Historia del teatro español.* Barcelona: Noguer, 1956. Finds fault with Martínez Sierra's static *costumbrista* pieces and favors the more active *Don Juan de España.*

2. Articles

ABAD, C. M. "La obra literaria de Martínez Sierra," *Razón y Fe,* 62 (1922), 177–95; on *Don Juan de España;* 63 (1922), 308–25, treats the early writings and novels; 64 (1925), 146–62, deals with the theater.

CROFTS, ERIK. "*El reino de Dios:* Two Commentaries," *Bulletin of Spanish Studies,* V, 18 (April 1928), 74–78. Comments on the Spanish play, the English translation, and the London stage production.

DOUGLAS, FRANCES. "Gregorio Martínez Sierra," *Hispania,* V, 5 (November 1922), 257–369 and VI, 1 (February 1923), 1–13. The most complete introduction to Martínez Sierra in article form.

ESPINOSA, AURELIO DE. Introduction to *Canción de cuna* (Boston: D.C. Heath and Co., 1921), ix–xxiv. Stresses the pantheism, poetic realism, and *españolismo* of Martínez Sierra.

——. Introduction to *Teatro de ensueño* (New York: World Book Co., 1920), xi–xvii. After describing the Spanish theatrical situation in the early twentieth century, Espinosa traces the development of Martínez Sierra to 1915. He classifies him as a nationalistic, neo-Romantic, and optimistic writer.

GARDNER, MAY. Introduction to *Sueño de una noche de agosto* (New York: Holt, Rinehart and Winston, 1921), vii–xxv. General survey of Gregorio Martínez Sierra's work; special attention to women characters in the theater.

HUSSON, MARGARET. Introduction to *Mamá*. (New York: W. W. Horton and Co., 1937), pp. 11–15. Stresses collaboration of Gregorio and María in more of an enumeration of their works than an introduction to them or to *Mamá*.

MASSA, PEDRO. "Los cien felices años de María Martínez Sierra," *Los domingos de ABC*, March 3, 1974, pp. 22–25. In remarkable possession of her mental facilities, María speaks of the past with the interviewer. Adds little to *Gregorio y yo*.

O'CONNOR, PATRICIA W. "La madre española en el teatro de Gregorio Martínez Sierra," *Duquesne Hispanic Review*. IV, I (1967), 17–24. A look at the conservative Spanish mother, antithesis of the idealization of maternity usually associated with the nun-mothers.

————. "A Spanish Precursor to Women's Lib: The Heroine in Gregorio Martínez Sierra's Theater," *Hispania*, LV, 4 (December 1962), 865–72. A study of the independent, feminist heroine.

ONIS, FEDERICO DE. Introduction to *Sol de la tarde* (Boston: D.C. Heath and Co., 1925), vii–xvii. Focuses on the poetic optimism of Martínez Sierra in the novels and stories.

OWEN, ARTHUR L. Introduction to *El ama de la casa* (Chicago: Benjamin H. Sonborn and Co., 1927), xi–xlv. Extensive and important review of Martínez Sierra's life and works up to 1921.

SALGADO, MARÍA A. "Teatro de ensueño: Colaboración modernista de Juan Ramón Jiménez y Gregorio Martínez Sierra," *Hispanófila*, 38 (January 1970), 49–58. Careful study; contrasts optimistic, vital subjects of Martínez Sierra with the theme of death chosen by Juan Ramón Jiménez.

STARKIE, WALTER. "Gregorio Martínez Sierra and Modern Spanish Drama," *Contemporary Review*, 125 (February 1924), 198–205. Rather general study of characters in the early plays.

UNDERHILL, JOHN GARRET. Introduction to *The Plays of Sierra*, I (London: Chatto and Windus, 1923), v–xix. Two lucid assessments of Martínez Sierra's theater by Underhill and H. Granville Barker.

YOUNG, RAYMOND A. "Benavente, Martínez Sierra y Ruben Darío: Una comparación," *Actas del congreso internacional de Hispanistas*. Mexico: Colegio de Mexico, 1970, pp. 935–44. Comparison of Benavente's *Rosas de otoño* with Martínez Sierra's *Primavera en otoño* with some reference to Rubén Darío's poem "Canción de otoño en primavera."

Index